Praise for *A Spirit Walker's Guide to Shama...*

"What I love about listening to Eve[...] [...]manism is her ability to combine ancient lore [...] science so seamlessly that you would swear you can't [...] one without the other. With the lyrical voice of an artist she taps into our memories of old, 'forgotten' ways and helps us understand them in terms of the latest findings in physics, psychology, and ecology. She is a wonderful guide for spirit walking between the worlds. Walk with her."

—TOM COWAN, author of *Fire in the Head* and *Yearning for the Wind*

"An inspiring and critically important work, this book helps you use all of the spiritual tools and connections you were born with, but most likely forgot. Spirit Walking clearly explains what shamanism is and does, while teaching in a concise, step-by-step fashion how to bring this way of being into your everyday life. I loved that I could feel the profound wisdom of many years of experience flow through Evelyn's writing in such a personal way. It feels like she is teaching you directly, with all her deeply rooted energy and spirit guided words. Whether you are new to shamanism, or are living this way of life already, you will find this book a valuable resource. At a time when life can seem so crazy, we need to become Spirit Walkers now, more than ever!"

—COLLEEN DEATSMAN, author of *The Hollow Bone: A Field Guide to Shamanism* and *Seeing in the Dark: Claim Your Own Shamanic Power Now and in the Coming Age.*

"*In our ever-changing world many people have felt lost and isolated within their lives, this statement is growing faster than we can keep up. Through Evelyn's Spirit Walking her grace and gifts are expressed to shift our connection to the earth, each other, and ourselves, building the foundation for life in a new and different world. She is an exceptional writer, artist, healer and human 'being.'*"

—JOAN EMMONS, publisher of *Inner Tapestry*

"*Evelyn Rysdyk brings the reader face to face with the bones of reality—how it works in this Middle World—and how the practice of shamanism helps us to live in good relationship with All That Is. Embracing the venerable world-view of shamanism she compassionately guides readers on their own journey of discovery and empowerment within the reality of an ensouled Universe. Spirit Walking is comprehensive and inspiring—Evelyn's outstanding artistry is evocatively expressed through her writings as well as images. A most worthy read!*"

—NAN MOSS AND DAVID CORBIN, authors of *Weather Shamanism: Harmonizing Our Connection with the Elements*

"*Evelyn Rysdyk has written an invaluable shamanic resource that is at once expansive and concise. She shares her deep wisdom with humility and great generosity of spirit.*"

—MAMA DONNA HENES, urban shaman, author, and spirituality columnist for the Huffington Post, Beliefnet and UPI

"*Life is a sacred work...how easy it is to forget that in the rush of daily life! And how wonderful it is when a book like [Spirit Walking] comes along, not only reminding us of our deepest sense of connection and purpose, but offering wise guidance to help us get back to it.*"

—HILLARY S. WEBB, author of *Traveling between the Worlds: Conversations with Contemporary Shamans*

A Spirit Walker's Guide to

Shamanic Tools

How to Make and Use
Drums, Masks, Rattles,
and Other Sacred Implements

A Spirit Walker's Guide to

Shamanic Tools

How to Make and Use
Drums, Masks, Rattles,
and Other Sacred Implements

EVELYN C. RYSDYK

WEISER BOOKS
San Francisco, CA / Newburyport, MA

First published in 2014 by Weiser Books
Red Wheel/Weiser, LLC
With offices at:
665 Third Street, Suite 400
San Francisco, CA 94107
www.redwheelweiser.com

ISBN: 978-1-57863-557-3

Library of Congress Cataloging-in-Publication Data available upon
request.

Cover design by Jim Warner.
Cover art © Evelyn C. Rysdyk.
Interior by Maureen Forys, Happenstance Type-O-Rama
Typeset in Warnock Pro and Futura

Printed in Canada.
MAR
10 9 8 7 6 5 4 3 2 1

This book is dedicated to the heart-guided hands of the hundred thousand generations of ancestral makers who created and utilized objects of spiritual power.

Their passion infuses our blood and bones.

Contents

Introduction   **xiii**

Chapter 1: The Rattle   **1**
   Exercise: Making a Rawhide Rattle   6
   Exercise: Journey to Empower Your New Rattle   13

Chapter 2: Bags and Containers   **17**
   Exercise: Making a Soft Leather Pouch   22
   Exercise: Beading the Edge of a Bag   31

Chapter 3: A Spirit Walker's Diagram of
Spiritual Connections   **35**
   Exercise: Making a Diagram of Your
      Spiritual World and Connections   41

Chapter 4: Creating a Shaman Tree   **47**
   Exercise: Dedicating the Shaman Tree   53

Chapter 5: The Drum   **59**
   Exercise: Making a Rawhide Frame Drum   73
   Exercise: Journeying to Empower Your Drum   75
   Exercise: Ulchi Drum Beats   82
   Exercise: Your Drum Beats   84

Chapter 6: Flutes and Whistles   87

    Exercise: Making a Bone Flute   91

    Exercise: Journey to Empower Your New Flute   96

    Exercise: Playing from the Heart   98

    Exercise: Making a Wooden Spirit Whistle   102

    Exercise: Journey to Empower Your New Whistle   106

Chapter 7: Prayer Beads and *Malas*   109

    Exercise: Making a Strand of Prayer Beads   116

Chapter 8: Bells   119

    Exercise: Choosing a Bell   122

    Exercise: Empowering Your Bell   123

Chapter 9: Shaman Bundles, Talismans, and Prayer Bundles   125

    Exercise: Creating a Spirit Bundle   132

    Exercise: Empowering Your Bundle   133

Chapter 10: Masks   135

    Exercise: Making Your Own Shamanic Fringe Mask   138

    Exercise: Empowering Your Fringe Mask   140

    Exercise: Making a Nature Spirit Mask   141

    Exercise: Empowering Your Nature Spirit Mask   144

Chapter 11: Shamanic Mirrors   147

    Exercise: Making a Shaman's Mirror   149

Chapter 12: Spirit Figures   151

    Exercise: Creating a Spirit Figure   155

Chapter 13: Feathers and Fans   159

    Exercise: Preparing a Bird Wing to Make a Fan   162

Chapter 14: Wands and *Phurbas*   167

Chapter 15: The Long Staff and Wind Staffs   177
     Exercise: Choosing a Shaman Staff   182
     Exercise: Empowering Your Staff   184
     Exercise: Making Wind Staffs   187
     Exercise: Using the Staffs for Healing Yourself   190

Chapter 16: Shamans' Costumes   193
     Exercise: Creating Ritual Clothing   202
     Exercise: Empowering Your Ritual Clothing   204

Conclusion   207

Appendix A: Tribal shamans mentioned in this book   209

Appendix B: Glossary of terms   213

Appendix C: Resources   223

Notes   227

Bibliography   233

About the Author   237

To Our Readers   238

Disclaimer

This book does not replace formal instruction in shamanic spirituality. It is necessary for you to know how to journey and have a strong connection to a power animal or teacher before you work with this book.

To learn more about shamanic journeying and developing relationships with the helpful, healing spirits, please read *Spirit Walking: A Course in Shamanic Power*.

The suggestions, processes, and shamanic techniques described in this book are in no way meant to replace professional medical or mental health assistance. This book is intended to be an informational guide and not to treat, diagnose, or prescribe. Always consult with a qualified health care professional regarding any medical or mental health condition or symptoms. Neither the author nor the publisher accepts any responsibility for your health or how you choose to use the information contained in this book.

Introduction

This volume was specifically designed to support those of you who have learned how to access the spirit realms through the shaman's journey and desire to add the right spiritual implements to your shamanic toolkit. If you picked up this book and don't yet know how to journey, you may learn what you need via several methods. There are several excellent books available that can guide you through the practice. Two outstanding resources for learning the shamanic journey process are my own book, *Spirit Walking: A Course in Shamanic Power*, and Sandra Ingerman's *Shamanic Journeying: A Beginner's Guide*. In addition, there are many teachers available to support you in person. The website *www.shamanicteachers. com* has a list of authorities across North America, Europe, and Australia. Information on my own initiatory shamanic training programs is available at *www.spiritpassages.com*. Spirit Passages is the organization I founded with my partner, Allie Knowlton, MSW, LCSW, DCSW to support individuals increase their personal power, feel their intrinsic sacredness, and expand their connections to All That Is. However you learn, take the time to strengthen your connections to the spirits prior to attempting the spiritual exercises in this book.

Learning to journey and having strong relationships with a teacher in the spirit world and with a protector spirit in the form of a power animal make up the basic framework for any effective shamanic practice. People who have gained this knowledge through their culture's tribal traditions are typically referred to as *shamans*. I will mention several of these tribal healers with whom I've been fortunate to study in this book. Their full biographies are available in an appendix. However, it is also possible for anyone without a tribal affiliation to become an effective shamanic practitioner or *spirit walker* by entering into deep relationships with the spirits. The foundation of any powerful shamanic work is dependent upon the relationships forged with the helpful spirits in the Upper, Middle, and Lower Worlds. Journeying to meet with the helpful spirits and following through with the guidance they offer sustains these relationships. Engaging with the spirits of nature is another essential aspect of becoming a powerful spirit walker. This aspect of practice is supported through journeying to meet the spirits of the trees, animal, birds, and landscape features around your home to find out who they are and what they might like to share. Just as with human connections, initial meetings blossom into reciprocal relationships that nurture the spirit walker and support the health of the natural world. My book *Spirit Walking: A Course in Shamanic Power* takes you through this process and provides the basics for becoming a truly powerful shamanic practitioner.

Whether you are looking at your connections to helping spirits or spirits of nature, you will find that certain objects facilitate those connections and support you to accomplish your work more easily. For instance, the sacred sounds of drums, rattles, and other implements accompany your spirit journeys. Power objects such as staffs, crystals, and masks amplify your intention, concretize that which is "invisible," or provide a stronger connection to power in your relationship with your helpful and healing spirits.

Navajo traditional healers bring rattles, corn pollen, eagle feathers, and sage smoke together with songs and dances to effect healing. An Ulchi shaman would need a drum, rattle, and larch wands called *gimsacha* to work healing magic. A Manchu shaman would need to perfume the air with incense and tie on a heavy bustle of iron jingles as a part of a ceremonial costume. Western-trained, core shamanic practitioners may utilize many different forms of ritual objects. Often contemporary practitioners have also been trained in one or more indigenous traditions which they incorporate as a part of their healing practice. The implements used are extensions of the shaman's intention and power. They support and/or magnify the connection with the helpful, healing spirits that guide the shaman's actions.

Archaeological evidence shows that we human beings have been making tools for at least 2.6 million years. Early in our development, we discovered that certain objects could help us accomplish tasks more easily. Our stone implements allowed us to hammer, drill, cut, and shape the details of our physical world.

By 40,000 years ago, we were using our tools to craft sophisticated musical instruments, as well as in drawing, painting, and carving figurines that assisted us in expressing complex ideas and our intangible feelings. Shamanic implements are an outgrowth of this progression as they support us to go deeper into the intangible worlds through journeys to the numinous realms of spirit. There, we navigate the complex interrelationships that are continually creating our physical existence.

My own early years were filled with an incredible array of tools, as my family elders were very creative. My mother and my great uncle expressed their talents in traditional paintings and drawings, but most of the others built structures, made household goods, and created what they needed to make their lives work. For them, tools were a part of solving the challenges of everyday life.

As the eldest child, I was often the designated helper for my father. Like others in my ancestral line, he was a creative man gifted with his hands. Along with being an amazing automobile mechanic who designed and built cars from the ground up, he was very talented at welding, carpentry, and numerous other forms of craftsmanship. His tool chests were filled with a variety of wrenches, pliers, saws, calipers, and other highly unique implements designed for very specific tasks. Through observing him at work, I quickly learned that these tools functioned like extensions of his hands. They assisted him in getting a job done.

On the other hand, while in art school I met highly skilled artists who could use a common ballpoint pen to create a masterpiece. Learning this lesson was equally important as I realized that while the right tool makes a task easier, it is critical to develop the skills to use each one first. Without the knowledge to wield them, tools are no more than fancy paperweights.

I have found the same to be true of shamanic implements. Finding the right drum will not make you a shaman. However, any drum in the hands of a skilled shamanic practitioner can be an object of power. It becomes inspirited—alive—and capable of assisting in the spirit walker's work. It provides the heartbeat of your journey, a way to accompany your spirit songs, a portal through which you can travel, and is capable of many other roles in your practice. The same may be said for all the other objects used by a true spirit walker. Each of them has a purpose and has been enlivened to become active partners in the shaman's work.

It is my belief that an extra dimension of power opens up when you craft your own tools. Working with the separate elements that will become the implement and the spirits in those elements deepens the spirit walker's connections to the final product. I also like knowing exactly what separate elements went into my tools. For instance, I know that the tiny pebbles in my favorite rattle came from the local riverbank, the handle is wood harvested from a lightning-struck maple in my yard, and the rawhide was once part of a Maine black bear hunted by a native friend for food. My having an intimate connection to all the spirits that came together in my rattle gives it a deeper meaning and power.

Of course, this is not to say that you *have* to make everything that you use in your shamanic practice! I use several shamanic tools that were either purchased or given to me by one of my indigenous teachers. If any project in this book seems too difficult, you may choose to purchase the implement discussed and then use the empowerment instructions to enliven your new power object. Once empowered, any tool will become a living partner in your work.

This book is designed to support those of you who are actively journeying to gather what you require to effectively and powerfully engage with the spirits. I believe that those of us following the shamanic path are the best hope for returning our human culture into wholeness. Spirit walkers know that everything is alive and sentient. We understand that all beings are precious and that we must consider their needs by staying in mutually beneficial relationships with them to maintain harmony. Through our journeys and with guidance from our loving tutelary spirits, we are helping to shape a more positive and healthy world.

EVELYN C. RYSDYK

CHAPTER 1

The Rattle

Since shamans receive much of their training and guidance from their tutelary spirits, the implements any particular shaman uses for healing are unique and usually vary widely from one shaman to the next. Native shamans may be bound by their tribal traditions to use particular rituals and bring certain objects into a healing ceremony, but even within those specific traditions many variations exist. Rattles are an important part of the shaman's tool kit and widely used around the globe. In this chapter you will find out how shamans work with rattles, and you will learn to create and empower your own rawhide rattle.

Some shamans use rattles much in the way drums would be, that is, to accompany the shamanic journey and keep shamans in the expanded state of consciousness required to perform their duties. Lighter and more portable than a drum, rattles can be used in situations when a drum may not be the best choice. For instance, a rattle is quieter and so may be the right implement when working indoors or when a softer sound would be beneficial. Rattles are also a great choice for working out in nature as they can be easily stashed in a backpack or coat pocket until they are needed. I find that I reach for my rattle as much as my drum to accompany my journeys. I often use it when I am doing shamanic work outdoors around my home so that I don't disturb my neighbors. The rattle is also my preferred shamanic instrument when I am engaging in healing work as I can be continuously rattling to keep myself in the shamanic state of consciousness at the same time I am using my other hand to work on my client.

A rawhide shaman's rattle is the first implement I have my students make in my initiatory shamanic training programs. It is a relatively easy object to create for people of all levels of crafting experience. This is the kind of rattle you will be guided through constructing in this chapter. However, there are as many variations among rattles as there are among drums. I have personally seen rattles constructed from gourds, buffalo or steer horn, turtle shells, rawhide, birch bark, animal hooves, bones, wood, seashells, and seedpods, among other materials. Some shamans even use objects such as tin cans or bottle caps as part of their rattles!

In North America, native tribal peoples use rattles extensively. In some cases the rattle replaces the drum as the primary shamanic instrument. Depending on the region, these may be made out of several different materials. Some rattles are fashioned from dried gourds that have been hollowed out, filled with a few small stones or seeds, and secured on a stick. Variations on this type of rattle are seen among the Northern and Eastern Woodlands, Plains, Southwestern, Californian, and Southern tribes of Native Americans. Especially large examples of these gourd rattles are made by the Hopi and other Pueblo peoples of the American Southwest. Some of the finest Hopi ceremonial rattles have been crafted from gourds with a round and slightly flattened shape like a fat disk. Usually very colorfully painted in combinations of white, black, yellow, red, turquoise, and green, these rattles have a feather secured by a string to the very top which flies around as the rattle is shaken.

Among the native people of the Great Plains of the United States, the gourds used are smaller and placed on a longer stick. Although these peoples traditionally leave the gourd head of the rattle undecorated, the handles are usually covered in designs of very beautiful and intricate beadwork.[1] Like the pueblo-style rattles, they too end in a feather at the top and often have a horsehair tail at the base of the handle. These elements add extra movement to the shaman's rattling gestures. The southern Pacific Coast and southwestern tribal peoples of the United States use gourd-shell rattles that are decorated by boring tiny holes across the surface of the head which have the effect of slightly amplifying the rattle's sound.[2]

Gourd rattles of the Cherokee utilize the neck of the gourd to create a handle. The gourd is carefully sliced at the base of the neck, the insides of the gourd are removed, pebbles are inserted, and then the neck is replaced with a small plug of wood providing a support to the joint. These rattles can be quite eccentrically shaped, based on the form in which the gourd originally grew.

Among the Guarani people of the Amazon forest, the rattle or *ubaraka mri*, is the tool the shaman uses to "communicate with god." The round gourd part of the rattle is seen as a womb and the handle as a penis. As such, the structure of the rattle helps to maintain the overall balance between masculine and feminine energies. Like the Hopi examples, these rattles also have feathers attached at the top that flutter as the rattle is shaken.[3]

I have held examples of African rattles that had heads made from a gourd with a forked stick for a handle. Wire was strung between the forked ends of the handle, and flattened bottle caps had been pierced and strung along the entire wire's length. This design makes a very effective rattle with a wonderfully loud, clashing sound when shaken, thanks to the combined nature of the sounds of the gourd and bottle caps. Indeed, as is the case with many Siberian and central Asian shamanic drumbeaters, the extra jingles produce a fine rhythmic rattling sound to accompany the shaman's work.

In places where gourds were not as common and the weather is damp, the native peoples turned other local materials to create their ceremonial rattles. The Woodland tribes famous for utilizing the magnificently beautiful bark of birch trees for food containers, storage vessels, and even their canoes also reached for this material in making their rattles. Using the bark from fallen trees, a cylinder is sewn together with the white or outside of the bark turned to the inside. A circular top and bottom were then fashioned and sewn to the ends of the tube after pebbles or dried corn kernels were placed inside. This made a shape somewhat like a tin can. A hole was then bored through the top and bottom ends so that a stick could be passed through the rattle and secured. Horn rattles are made in this same manner by simply replacing the birch bark tube with a section of buffalo or steer horn. The Eastern Woodlands people are known for their rattles made of turtle shells. Beautiful examples of these may be found at powwows across New England and into eastern Canada. Using the empty turtle shell as the container for pebbles or seeds, these rattles sometimes incorporate an actual turtle head as a part of the rattle.

Among the people of North America's Pacific Coast, wood has also been the primary resource for making a shaman's rattle. Surrounded by the enormous trees of the temperate rain forest, these peoples are known for utilizing wood in both everyday and sacred objects as well as for their extraordinarily fine carvings. Originally the shaman's rattles were round in overall shape and carved over their surface with images of the shaman's spiritual helpers.[4]

Sometimes the figures that form the rattle are quite fierce-faced. These effigy-like carvings may be empowered by the shaman so that they become extensions of the shaman's power or function as partners during healing work. Other Northwest Coast rattles are quite elaborately carved into the shape of the animals they represent and often also carefully painted. Particularly fine examples of these figure rattles are found among the Tlingit people. Rattles have been carved to resemble oystercatchers, ravens, bears, and other totemic animals. A dear friend who is a shamanic practitioner in Quebec uses a particularly fine example of this type of rattle in her healing practice. She works with Raven, and the rattle is carved in a wonderfully stylized image of this spirit's head.

Figure 1. Tsimshian shaman's rattle. (Pen and ink © 2013 Evelyn C. Rysdyk)

Animal rawhide is another common material for rattle making. Rawhide becomes very flexible when soaked in water and can be easily shaped while in that pliable state. Once dry, the rawhide becomes quite hard again and provides a nice sound. The most commonly seen rawhide rattle is created by sewing wet rawhide into a sack or container-like shape, which is filled with sand to hold its form until dry. Once the head of the rattle is hard again, the resulting hollow is emptied of sand, filled with seeds, beads, crystals, or pebbles, and secured to a handle. This basic formula can be used to make rattles of many different shapes. The Sioux of the Great Plains and Ojibwa of the northern central woodlands of the United States and southern Canada often make rattles in a shape similar to maracas. The latter people sometimes pierce their rattle heads in the manner of the Papago tribe of the Sonoran Desert.

In truth, rattles have been made from just about anything that produces noise, even pieces of antler, deer hooves, puffin beaks, and bones. Shamans have ingeniously exploited every available resource to provide the sounds necessary to support their journeys into the spirit realms.

Exercise: Making a Rawhide Rattle

To become an effective shamanic practitioner or spirit walker, it is important to take opportunities to concretize the lessons you receive from spirit. When a spiritual lesson is manifested in this reality, it allows you to more fully internalize what you have learned. You will feel the work more deeply and strengthen the connections with your helping spirits.

Indeed, performing a ceremony such as making a gratitude offering or honoring the spirits of the natural world supports you in becoming more powerful. Another method for making the spiritual experience more physical is to create some of the objects you will be using as a spirit walker. This is one of the reasons I have always included making objects in Spirit Passages training programs.

While you may have many other shamanic implements over the course of your life, the simple rattle you will create in this exercise can become a powerful part of your practice. I have many rattles that I have purchased—most of which are more elegantly made than my own. However, the one that I crafted myself has become so empowered through my constructing and using it that its efficacy for me far exceeds the others.

Materials and Tools

- A piece of rawhide about twelve inches square and an eighth of an inch thick

- A stick for a handle

- Sandpaper

- A PDF file of the full-sized, full-color rattle pattern and instructions found here may be downloaded at *www.myspiritwalk.com* (Print out two copies of your pattern and set one aside. This second copy will be a useful reference for the project in chapter 2.)

- A soft pencil

- A good, sharp pair of scissors

- A push awl or sharp nail the same thickness as your needle

- A hammer

- A rectangular piece of scrap plywood or other flat board such as a secondhand cutting board about ten to twelves inches or so across (You will be putting holes in this piece.)

- A spool of artificial sinew

- A needle that is big enough to thread the sinew

- Two large skeins of natural, undyed, *thick* wool knitting yarn or wool roving (unspun wool that has been cleaned and combed)

- An embroidery hook to remove wool when the rattle is dry

- One teaspoon or two of very tiny pebbles (one-sixteenth to one-eighth of an inch in diameter)

- White glue

- Drill and one-eighth-inch drill bit

- Small scrap of deerskin or other soft leather

- Paint, beads, feathers, and other things you may want to use to decorate your finished rattle

- A shamanic journey drumming recording with callback signal to facilitate your journeys to the spirits of the hide and handle as well as for empowering the rattle once it is completed

Rawhide is the scraped and dried hide of an animal. It is typically used for drumheads and may be found through companies that supply drum-making supplies. Commercial rawhide is usually from a steer, but it is possible to find deer, elk, goat, and even black bear rawhide through online sources. In a pinch, the larger ten-inch rawhide dog chews with the knot at each end may be used for a rattle. Choose only the unflavored variety to make your rattle!

Take time to pick out a handle stick with meaning for you and prepare it by sanding it smooth. If you are close to the ocean you may wish to use driftwood. Perhaps a beaver stick from a pond or river may appeal to you. You may ask your favorite tree for a small branch. Maybe you have a treasured piece of wood from building a house or piece of furniture. Even a dowel from the hardware store can be decorated to feel "just right!"

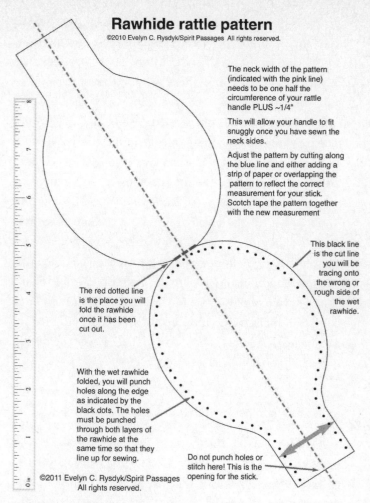

Rawhide rattle pattern

The neck width of the pattern (indicated with the pink line) needs to be one half the circumference of your rattle handle PLUS ~1/4"

This will allow your handle to fit snuggly once you have sewn the neck sides.

Adjust the pattern by cutting along the blue line and either adding a strip of paper or overlapping the pattern to reflect the correct measurement for your stick. Scotch tape the pattern together with the new measurement

This black line is the cut line you will be tracing onto the wrong or rough side of the wet rawhide.

The red dotted line is the place you will fold the rawhide once it has been cut out.

With the wet rawhide folded, you will punch holes along the edge as indicated by the black dots. The holes must be punched through both layers of the rawhide at the same time so that they line up for sewing.

Do not punch holes or stitch here! This is the opening for the stick.

Figure 2. Rawhide rattle pattern

Make the Rattle

1. Begin by gathering all of your tools and ingredients. Take time to make thoughtful choices. In planning a time to actually construct your rattle, remember that your piece of rawhide will have to be soaked in water overnight for it to be pliable.

2. While your rawhide soaks, you have the opportunity to sand and decorate your handle. Before you begin, perform an offering to thank all the spirits who are participating in the project with you. These include the animal whose hide you will be using, the tree from which the stick has come, and so on. Your offering can be as simple as burning incense while holding these spirits in your mind or placing a bit of cornmeal outside while saying your thanks aloud. Or you can reference the more extensive instructions in *Spirit Walking: A Course in Shamanic Power.* By entering into a prayerful state, you are inviting the spirits to participate with you. You may then wish to journey to find out what imagery or colors would be best for the handle. I like to use a wood-burning tool to decorate my rattle handles, as the designs hold up well over time. A combination of paint and incised lines produced through wood-burning can create wonderful handle designs. Whatever you decide is best for you will be just perfect!

3. On the day you will be assembling your rattle, gather your tools and again perform an offering to thank all the spirits.

4. You will notice that the pattern tells you to measure your handle's circumference. You can use the ruler that is on the pattern for this purpose. Adjust the pattern's neck according to the directions and then start tracing the pattern onto the rawhide's rough side (wrong side) with your soft pencil.

5. Carefully cut the pattern out of the rawhide.

6. Once your rawhide has been cut out, fold it along the line (red in the downloadable pattern) where the heads of the two bulbs meet and begin to punch the holes with your scrap plywood underneath your rawhide. A nail and hammer work equally well as a traditional leather punch for this purpose. Punch the holes about three-sixteenths of an inch

from the edge of the rawhide, starting at one side of the neck. *Only punch four or five at a time, then begin sewing.* If you try to punch more all at once, it may be difficult to align the holes when stitching.

7. Start sewing at one side of the neck leaving a tail of artificial sinew at the beginning of your stitches. I have found that using a stitch that goes over the edge seems to make the best looking finished rattle.

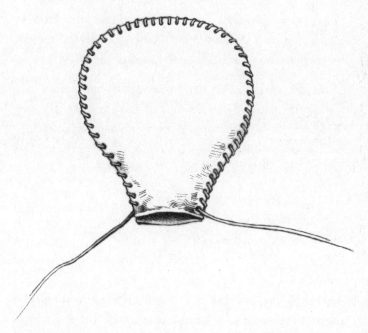

Figure 3. Leave tails at the beginning and end of your sewing. (Steps 7–9)

8. Complete the way around the rattle and again leave a long tail.

9. Start another length of sinew and sew again through the same holes from the other direction, remembering to leave tails at both ends. The result will be that the stitches cross over the outside seam. This will produce a nice finished outer edge on the rattle head.

10. Start stuffing the damp rawhide with wool. Keep feeding in the wool to make the rattle head round. You can use a smooth stick to force more of the wool into the rattle's opening. It will take more wool to stuff the rattle than you might believe is possible!

11. Temporarily place your stick in the neck of the rattle and leave it to dry in a sunny spot or put it in a *very* low oven (the lowest setting) for an hour or two to speed up the process.

12. Once the rawhide is hard and dry, remove the stick and take out all the wool. An embroidery hook is the perfect tool for coaxing the wool back out of the head of the rattle.

13. Put your stones inside the hollow and again temporarily replace the handle to test the sound. Experiment with more or fewer stones until it sounds best. (Remember, the sound will sharpen and become a bit louder as the rawhide dries even more thoroughly.)

14. Once you are happy with your sound, place a little bit of white glue in the neck and fit the stick in whatever you decide is to be its final orientation.

15. Let the glue dry.

16. Once the glue is completely dry, drill a hole through the neck of the rattle and the part of the stick that is inside.

17. Take the tails of your stitching sinew and thread them through the hole and tie them tightly. This further secures the rattle head to the stick.

18. Trim away any remaining tails of sinew.

19. Cut a length of soft leather. Wind and glue it around the neck to cover the knots you have just made.

20. At this point, you may decorate your finished rattle with beads, paint, or feathers.

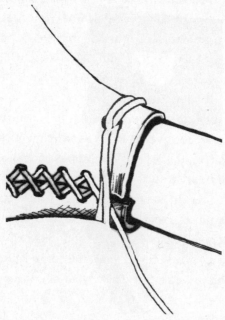

Figure 4. The tails of the stitching sinew go through the hole you drilled in the neck and are tied to secure the head of the rattle to the handle. Also visible here are the crossed stitches created by sewing in both directions as is explained in step 9.

Exercise: Journey to Empower Your New Rattle

At this point, your rattle needs to be enlivened and empowered for its sacred purpose. This is accomplished through a shamanic journey to your power animal, the protective spirit that provides guidance, healing, and many other benefits. If you haven't yet connected with a power animal, do a shamanic journey to the Lower World to meet yours prior to taking this empowerment journey.

When you are ready to dedicate your new rattle to your spirit walker practice, make a gratitude offering to the spirits. Honor that which you have been given and your connections to the world of spiritual power. Call with your heart to bring your power animal to you. When you feel ready, merge with the animal and begin to sing your power song while holding the rattle in your dominant hand. Shake the rattle with the rhythm of your song. Sing until you feel your song and your spiritual power extending into the rattle. When the process feels complete, shake your rattle to the rhythm of the journey callback signal, unmerge from your power animal, and return yourself to ordinary reality.

Upon your return to ordinary consciousness, take ample time to sit with the experience prior to recording it in your notebook. Remember to go outside and make an offering of thanks. Let your heart fill with gratitude for the gifts you have received in this experience and place your offering on the Earth with reverence.

Caring for Your Rattle

At this point you have a sacred object that has become an inspirited and therefore living being. Do a journey to your teacher or power animal and ask for suggestions for how you can care for the spirit of your rattle. For instance, the spirit of your rattle may require "feeding" with cornmeal, scented water, essential oil, or even tobacco.

As to ordinary reality care, keep your rattle dry and store it in a secure place. Always put it away after working with it. Never leave it lying on the floor, especially if you have a dog. Your rattle began its life as a piece of rawhide and a stick, and your dog will continue to view it that way! You may also want to find or make a bag to carry it safely when you are working outdoors.

Journey Explorations

- Journey to a teacher or power animal to ask: "What are the ways I am to use this rattle in my shamanic practice?" Record the content of your journey and your perceptions about what you receive.

- Journey to a teacher or power animal to ask: "What is the best way to care for my rattle's spirit?"

After each journey, remember to make an offering to the spirits.

Process Questions

- Write down in your journal what it was like to create a rattle.

- How does it feel to have this special tool support your process? Record your impressions.

CHAPTER 2

Bags and Containers

Since your new rattle is a sacred, empowered object for your spiritual practice, it is living and requires care. Just as your helper spirits have homes in the Upper, Lower, or Middle World, your empowered objects must have appropriate places to reside. You will also need to carry your rattle along as you work in other places and out in nature. For this reason, it is important to have an appropriate bag or container to hold your rattle.

All of the sacred objects you will gather in your practice will require suitable "homes." By putting a tool "away" when you are finished with it, you are honoring that it is a sacred implement dedicated for a specific purpose rather than an ordinary household object. By making it a place to reside you further concretize the awareness of it as a living being.

Indeed, some of a spirit walker's containers can develop power of their own. The late Tuvan shaman Ai Churek had many objects, bags, and containers on her altar. Each of these had been empowered and could perform healings on her patients. Her rattle, drum, drumbeater, staff, charm bags, and other objects all had their own spirits, which allowed her to work with a large group of people by both attending to them in person and placing her objects on those that may have required extra support from the spirits. She had several small charm bags that she termed *ehrens*, or spirit protectors, in that they held not only objects but a living spirit as well. These could be hung on a door, placed in a car, or worn on the body and functioned as both guardians and healers. In fact, Ai Churek had several of these small spirit bags sewn to the surface of her coat, which augmented her spiritual power and protected her as she worked.

Figure 5. Ai Churek in costume. (Photo: Carl A. Hyatt)

Shamans from different cultures use a variety of materials to hold their sacred objects. The First Peoples of North America made containers out of leather, rawhide, bark, wood, horn, clay, and bone. These substances would have been readily available in their environment, and skilled artisans were able to produce objects that were both useful and beautiful for storage. In many regions, highly talented native craftspeople still create incredibly beautiful versions of these once common objects. The most exquisite examples are shown in museums and fine craft galleries, often fetching high prices for the talented women and men who make them.[5]

On the Pacific Northwest Coast, trees are resources used extensively by traditional native peoples. The wood from cedars is durable, easy to carve, and resistant to both rotting and insect damage. It is also easy to split into boards from which boxes and trunks may be made. These boxes would be decorated with carved and painted images of the shaman's protective spirits and clan affiliations. Along with the wood, other parts of the cedar were also employed. For instance, the inner bark has a straight grain with long, strong fibers that may be either woven into a bark cloth or twisted into fine cordage, which can then be coiled and sewn into baskets, hats, and other garments. These objects and containers are flexible but very durable and incredibly fragrant.

Figure 6. Early 19th-century Haida box of carved western yellow cedar held together with spruce roots and animal sinew. (Pen and ink © 2013 Evelyn C. Rysdyk)

Wherever birch trees grow, indigenous people have made good use of them. Aspects of the birch can serve as an analgesic medicine, tar made from the bark's oil is a durable glue, and the high tannin content of the inner bark makes it ideal for tanning animal hides into leather. Often gathered as a fire-starting tinder, birch bark is also strong, durable, water-resistant, and easily cut, bent, and sewn, making it a valuable commodity for building structures, producing objects such as canoes, and crafting containers. Birch bark also contains *betulin*—a substance that has fungicidal properties. As a result, food that is stored in birch bark containers is better preserved. Indeed, both household and sacred containers made from birch bark have been found in cultures as varied as Arctic Scandinavia, Siberia, the Russian Far East, and the North American continent.

Figure 7. Orochi birch bark basket from the Khabarovsk region of Siberia in Russia. (Pen and ink ©2013 Evelyn C. Rysdyk)

Among the Eastern Woodlands peoples of North America, the bark of birch trees was commonly used to create flat winnowing baskets for separating kernels of grain from their inedible husks, square baskets, and beautiful round boxes with lids. Either the white side faced out to show off the decorative bark of the tree, or the reddish-brown inner bark was put on the exterior so that it could be scratched away to create intricate designs.

The Wabanaki peoples of New England and Maritime Canada—including the Penobscot, Passamaquoddy, Maliseet, Mi'kmaq, and Abenaki peoples—produced birch bark containers, too. However, they are perhaps better known for their extremely fine, brown ash splint baskets. These containers are beautiful, practical, long-wearing, and still as useful today as they were centuries ago. My partner's grandmother was a Penobscot basket maker. We have a few examples of her work from the early 1900s that we still use in our home. Today, native basket making is recognized as a fine craft skill by the wider culture, and as a result this tradition is being preserved. There are several fine basket makers working among Maine's Wabanaki people, and thanks to organizations such as the Maine Indian Basketmakers Alliance, the native weavers are able to preserve and pass on this skill to future generations. Some sites to visit with explanations of methods and fine examples of this craft are those of Penobscot basket maker Barbara D. Francis (*www.penobie.com*) and Passamaquoddy weaver Deborah Gabriel Brooks (*www.sweetgrassbasketry.org*). Examples of the work of Maliseet basket maker Fred Tomah can also be found online.

Along with making birch bark boxes and brown ash split baskets, the Wabanaki have also traditionally braided extremely long ropes of native sweetgrass (*Hierochloe odorata*), which were then coiled into beautiful, aromatic baskets. This technique is used in Maine and the Canadian Maritimes. As one travels south along the Eastern Seaboard and inland to the Great Plains, you can find tribal people using wrapped bunches of sweetgrass instead of braids. Bunches of needles from several species of pine are also gathered in a similar fashion to make coil baskets.

You may already be familiar with the small leather pouches some people wear around their necks to hold tiny sacred objects. Native American in origin, these medicine bags have become very popular in the broader culture as well. A leather bag is soft against the skin and gentle to whatever is contained within it. Wherever deer, elk, or caribou are found the indigenous peoples used their skins for clothing and bags to hold food, tools, tobacco, and other necessary items. In my experience, soft leather is one of the best materials for bags of all sizes. It is gentle enough to protect delicate objects and still durable enough to last for many years.

The native peoples of North America also decorated their leather bags with beadwork. The peoples of the Eastern Woodlands created beautiful floral designs while those of the Great Plains favored elaborate geometric patterns. The glass beads were not only pretty but also helped to protect the outer surface of the bag from wear. Once decorated in this manner, a bag can last for decades or in some cases many generations.

Across Siberia, leather bags are also an important part of a shaman's ritual paraphernalia. Usually crafted from reindeer leather, these containers house small fetishes, healing herbs, special stones or crystals, the shaman's rattle, and other sacred objects. Small bags filled with herbs or little figures could also be sewn onto a shaman's costume. In these cases, the bags function as vehicles carrying the spirits that accompany a shaman during her or his work.

Exercise: Making a Soft Leather Pouch

These instructions are for a pouch that is styled like the traditional "coffee bag" used by the Sami people of Arctic Scandinavia, which can be sized to fit your rattle. While a Sami craftsperson would construct a bag from birch bark-tanned reindeer leather, yours may be made out of any thin and flexible leather typically used for garments or upholstery. The smooth and soft leathers of a lamb, pig, or goat all make excellent bags that are easy to sew. Deerskin can also be a good choice even though it is a bit heavier and a little more difficult to stitch. Hides can be either smooth leather or suede; either one will make a lovely bag. You may run across deer or cowhide leather advertised as a "split" or "split hide." This is leather which has been divided to make it a thinner weight. It essentially creates two hides: one with a smooth side and a suede reverse and another with two suede surfaces. The smooth side of a piece of leather is the side that was once the hairy side of the skin. In the tanning process, the fur of the animal was removed.

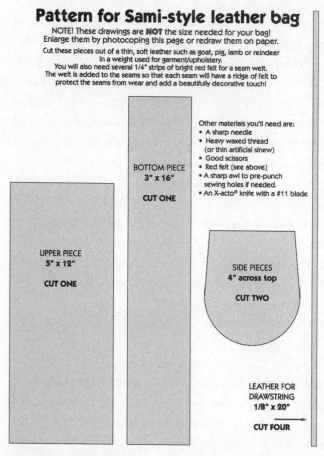

Pattern for Sami-style leather bag

NOTE! These drawings are **NOT** the size needed for your bag!
Enlarge them by photocoping this page or redraw them on paper.

Cut these pieces out of a thin, soft leather such as goat, pig, lamb or reindeer in a weight used for garment/upholstery.
You will also need several 1/4" strips of bright red felt for a seam welt.
The welt is added to the seams so that each seam will have a ridge of felt to protect the seams from wear and add a beautifully decorative touch!

BOTTOM PIECE
3" x 16"

CUT ONE

Other materials you'll need are:
• A sharp needle
• Heavy waxed thread
  (or thin artificial sinew)
• Good scissors
• Red felt (see above)
• A sharp awl to pre-punch
  sewing holes if needed.
• An X-acto® knife with a #11 blade

UPPER PIECE
5" x 12"

CUT ONE

SIDE PIECES
4" across top

CUT TWO

LEATHER FOR
DRAWSTRING
1/8" x 20"

CUT FOUR

Figure 8. Sami bag pattern

Your particular bag could be a combination of leather and suede, leather and fur, leather and wool, or have several different materials incorporated into the finished product. You can choose to cut one or both of the sidepieces of the pattern from a different color leather, colorful wool fabric, or piece of tanned fur. Whatever you decide, just make sure the sides are as flexible as the leather you are using for the rest of the pouch.

The template here was designed to be enlarged to fit your rattle; however, you can also use the template as is or at any other size you desire for holding other shamanic objects. I have laid out the bag so that it just covers the head of the rattle. If you also want to have the handle of your rattle in the bag, you will need to adjust the pattern so that the dimensions of the upper piece will be at least one inch deeper than the length of your handle. For instance, if your rattle has a nine inch handle, the upper piece may need to measure ten inches by twelve inches to accommodate it. A printable file of the pattern, which can be enlarged or reduced to the perfect size for your project, may be found at *www.myspiritwalk.com*.

Take your time with this project. If your bag doesn't turn our perfectly the first time, make another until you are happy with the results. I have found that every bag I make, even those that didn't turn out as I intended, winds up holding a sacred object. I use bags to hold my rattles, my healing tools, cornmeal for offerings, crystals, and for many other purposes. No bag ever stays empty for long!

Read all the instructions carefully before you begin.

Materials and Tools

- A piece of soft, garment or upholstery-weight leather (or wool or fur) that is big enough to accommodate your personalized leather pouch template

- A photocopy of the pattern sheet in the size you have chosen

- A soft pencil

- A good, sharp pair of scissors

- A sheet of red or another color felt cut into long, quarter-inch-wide strips (These will be sewn into every seam of your pouch. While the Sami traditionally use red or yellow, you may choose a color that is pleasing to you and that complements your chosen leather.)

- A spool of heavy, waxed "carpet" thread or artificial sinew that has been split to make the strands thinner

- A needle big enough for your chosen thread or sinew

- A push awl or sharp nail the same thickness as your needle

- A hammer if you have chosen thicker leather for your pouch

- A rectangular piece of scrap plywood or another flat board about ten to twelve inches across (You may use the same piece you used to make your rattle since you will also be putting holes in it.)

- An X-ACTO©-type craft knife with a #11 blade

- A paper clip

- Masking tape

- Felt, beads, or talismanic objects such as animal bones, claws, or teeth to decorate your finished bag (Use discretion when acquiring the parts of any animal or bird. Make sure it has been killed in an ethical manner and that the animal claw, bone, or tooth you plan to use is legal for you to own.)

Making Your Pouch

1. On the day that you plan to make your pouch, gather your right-sized pattern, tools, leather, and other materials.

Before you begin working, perform an offering to thank all the spirits. Especially honor the animal whose hide or fur you have chosen.

2. When you are ready to begin, trace your pattern onto the wrong size of your leather, wool, or fur.

3. Carefully use scissors to cut out all the pieces for your pouch. You will need two sidepieces, one bottom piece, and one upper piece. You will also need four one-eighth-inch strips of leather about twenty inches long to make a drawstrings. Also cut out the quarter-inch strips of felt you will use as seam welts.

4. You will need to whipstitch the long edges of the bottom strip to gather these. This will have the effect of puckering up the edges. The goal is to make the length of the bottom strip match the outside curves of the sidepieces.

5. Sew the upper piece into a tube with the right sides inside and a felt welt in the seam.

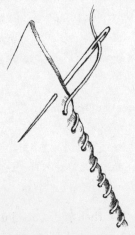

Figure 9. Sew a whipstitch along the edges of the bottom strip. Gather it as you sew so the strip puckers up, shortening it to match the outside radius of the sidepiece.

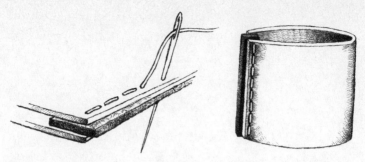

Figures 10 and 11. Sew the felt into the seam. The final piece will be a tubular shape.

6. You are now ready to begin assembling the pouch. Place one long edge of the bottom strip on one of the sidepieces with the felt welt sandwiched in between. Arrange the side and bottom pieces so that the right side of the leather—the side that you have decided will be the finished outside of your pouch—is facing inward.

7. Begin sewing. (If you have chosen thicker leather, you may need to use the hammer and awl to create holes so that sewing will be easier.) Sew your stitches one at a time no more than an one-eighth of an inch from the edge. Pull them snuggly and make them small and close enough together so that six to eight of your stitches would fit within an inch. Take your time with this!

8. Repeat this process with the other sidepiece.

9. Turn the pouch so that it is right side out.

10. Take your upper piece and sew the short sides to the right side of the leather inside.

11. With its right side still inside, slide the tube-shaped upper over the pouch. Sew the upper piece and pouch together with another felt welt in the seam. Take your time, being careful not to sew the front and back of your bag together!

Figure 12. Sew the sidepiece to the puckered bottom strip with a felt welt in the seam.

12. When you've finished sewing, turn the upper piece right side out by rolling it up into position.

13. Now it is time to make a closure for your pouch with a piece of primitive cordage from leather.

14. Place two of your leather strips side by side. Tie them together at one end leaving three-quarter-inch "tails." Anchor the knot in something that doesn't move. I find that closing the knotted end in a door or a drawer works quite well for this step.

15. Twist each strip counterclockwise as you ply them together in a clockwise direction. This takes a little bit of practice, so be patient with the process. This skill for making cordage was essential for our ancient ancestors, who used the results in snares, traps, and nets and to make thread. I find the act of plying cords connects me with the spirits of my deep ancestors.

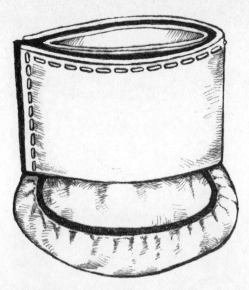

Figure 13. With the upper piece still inside out, sew it to the pouch, which is right side out. Make sure to sandwich a felt welt in the seam.

16. Keep twisting until you have made cordage from all but the last inch of the strips.

17. Now knot the final end of the cord.

18. Repeat these steps with the other two strips of leather.

19. You may now choose to tie the bag by wrapping the top with your cords *or* you may go on to the next step to make a drawstring hem on your pouch.

20. To create a drawstring sleeve, turn the entire pouch inside out. Fold down one inch of the upper piece. Carefully stitch the resulting tube as you did the other seams, being careful not to inadvertently sew the front and back of the bag together!

21. Turn the pouch right side out again.

22. Using your X-ACTO© craft knife, *carefully* slice small holes in the drawstring tube on the left and right sides, being

careful not to cut through the back of the tube or through any of your stitching.

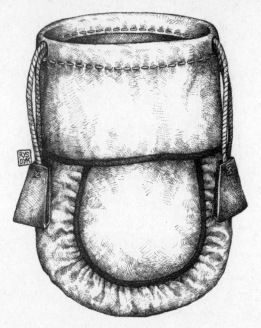

Figure 14. Drawstring bag

23. Straighten the paper clip and thread it through one of the knotted ends of your cord. Tape it in place so that it forms a "needle" with which you can thread the cord through the drawstring tube.

24. Thread one cord in from the left side all around the tube so it exits the same hole. Knot the two ends together.

25. Repeat the same step but thread this cord through the hole on the right side. Thread it all around the tube so it exits the same right-side hole and knot the ends together.

26. When the left cord and right cords are pulled, they will draw the bag closed.

27. Whether you have chosen to close your pouch by wrapping it in one cord or have created a drawstring, you may wish to sew a tab of leather or wool to each of the ends of the cord to finish it off.

28. Decorate your bag with the embellishments you have gathered, or see the next exercise for instructions on how to bead the edge of your bag.

When you have completed your pouch, you may wish to bless it with the fragrant smoke of sweetgrass, cedar, dried pine needles, sage, or your favorite incense. You may also choose to empower it as you did your rattle. Your finished pouch may hold your rattle or some of your other sacred objects, herbs, tobacco, or anything else that would complement your spirit walking practice. Based upon your needs, you can reduce or enlarge the pouch template to make bags of various different sizes.

This style pouch is just one of many possible bags you can make. A sheet with ideas for bags of different shapes may be found at *www.myspiritwalk.com*.

Many of the bags and pouch designs presented on the idea sheet can be enhanced through beadwork. An easy way to add color and texture to a leather or cloth pouch is to add beads along the edge of the opening. The following instructions and diagrams can help you to decorate your sacred bags and pouches.

Exercise: Beading the Edge of a Bag

Make a decorative edge for the opening of your bag or on the outside seams.

Materials and Tools

- Seed beads in at least two different colors that complement each other and the leather or fabric of your pouch or bag

- A sharp needle that easily passes through the opening of your beads while it is threaded

- A spool of thread or very thin beading cord

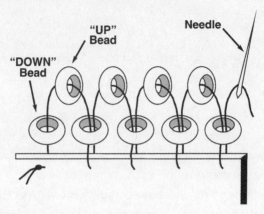

Figure 15. Diagram of beading an edge

Beading the Edge of Your Pouch

1. As you have done before, prepare yourself and your space for the work by making an offering and inviting in helping healing spirits.

2. Using the figure (above), begin sewing beads to the edge of the pouch. (If you are beading the pouch you made with the previous directions, make sure that the beading stitches do not interfere with your drawstring.) The upper beads will ride over the beads closest to the edge of the bag creating a "ruffled" look. Alternating bead colors can make your design more interesting.

3. Do at least six couplets and appraise your progress. If you like the look of the "ruffle," keep sewing. If you would prefer to try any of the effects in the variations of figure 16, pull out your stitches and start on something different. Remember the only one you have to please with your efforts is yourself!

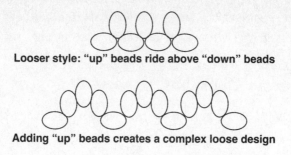

Looser style: "up" beads ride above "down" beads

Adding "up" beads creates a complex loose design

Tighter style: space out stitches to
place the "up" beads between the "down" beads

Figure 16. Beading variations

4. When you are finished with your beading, tie off the thread and clip the excess.

5. As you did when you first finished your pouch, bless the beadwork and yourself with sweetgrass, sage, or incense.

6. When you are through, put your sacred objects into the pouch and place it on your altar. Make a gratitude offering for all of your blessings and the assistance of the spirits.

Journey Explorations

- Journey to a teacher or power animal to ask: "What are the ways I am to use this pouch in my shamanic practice?" Record the content of your journey and your perceptions about what you receive.

- If you decided to empower your pouch, it is now a living being that requires special care. Journey to a teacher or power animal to ask: "What is the best way to care for my pouch's spirit?"

- Ask the spirit of your rattle or any other object you will keep in the pouch what it feels about its new home.

After each journey, make an offering to the spirits of nature, the animal that provided the leather, and your helping spirits.

Process Questions

- Write down in your journal what it was like to create a "home" for your rattle or other sacred objects.

- Consider what home means to you. Record your thoughts and feelings in your journal.

CHAPTER 3

A Spirit Walker's Diagram of Spiritual Connections

Spiritual art can provide a helpful bridge between our sensory world and the intangible world of the spirits. Shamanic art serves the same purpose. Like Eastern Orthodox icons, images of the spirits and their realms can provide a constant reminder of the guidance, support, and love the spirits offer. In essence, this kind of artwork allows us to feel the spirits' presence in our everyday life. These images can also provide a space for our helping spirits to reside in our world and function as a portal for our own shamanic journeywork. Whether executed as representational paintings or as more cryptic diagrams, these images can become a powerful part of a shaman's paraphernalia. Once fully inspirited, these maps or diagrams may act as part of a shaman's protection, support healing work, create a sacred space, or be used in divination rituals.

Across Siberia and into Arctic Europe, traditional shamans decorate their drums with representations of their helping spirits and spiritual realms. These shamanic diagrams allow the spirits who support the shaman to have a home in our reality. This means that the spirits are always nearby and so readily available to assist in shamanic work.

A drum might have paintings either on the playing surface or inside near the handle. In Siberia the handles themselves might also be carved in the shape of a spirit effigy, or *ongon*, that echoes the paintings on the drum skin. The drawing in Figure 18 is a painting from the inside of an Altai shaman's drum.

Figure 17. A map of a shaman's journey realms from central Siberia. (Pen and ink ©2013 Evelyn C. Rysdyk)

The central figure strongly resembles the handle of another Altai drum depicted in the chapter on spirit figures. The figure has wings, which reflect the shaman's ability to spiritually fly through the realms. Shamans' costumes across Siberia have fringes along the sleeves, hem, and back to represent this power and are also said to assist the shaman's spirit in soaring.

Surrounding the central figure are others that represent animals, plants, and celestial spirits. By depicting these helping spirits from nature and the heavens on the drum, the shaman provides a temporary "home" for them in the drum. This makes it easier for the spirits to work in our realm.

The figures on the Altai drum bear a striking resemblance to a Sami drum in the British Museum. This example also has two distinct designs with different images, but as you are able to see the same theme of a central figure surrounded by spirits is plainly visible.

Figure 18. Painted images from the inside of an Altai shaman's drum. The central figure also mimics the vertical axis of the World Tree that unites the spiritual realms. (Pen and ink ©2013 Evelyn C. Rysdyk)

The Example of a Sami *Noaidi*'s Drum

Sami drums, or *goavdi* (*runebomme* in Norwegian), are typically painted with a diagram of the *noaidi's* helping spirits, her or his powerful places in the spiritual realms, nature deities, important people, herd animals, domestic objects, and other images that are personal to the shaman. Typical animal representations include images of *heargi* (reindeer), *rieben* (fox), *guovza* (bear), *vourccis* (crow), and other species found in the Sami homeland.

Also included on the shaman's drum would be anthropomorphic representations of normally faceless forces of nature such as the sun, the winds, fertility, water, and the Earth.

Figure 19. 17th-century *goavdi* from northern Norway. The vertical element that slices the sun resembles the Altai drum's imagery. (Permanent collection of the British Museum. Digital illustration © 2013 Evelyn C. Rysdyk)

The humanlike forms made these impossibly large spirits more accessible for relationship and so more easily allowed communication with them. These "gods and goddesses" might include the Earth Mother Maderáhkká and her three daughters who watched over the home, women, children, and all family life; Laib olmai who watched over all the animals in the forest and so was responsible for bestowing luck upon a hunter; and Horagalles, the god of thunder. A figure representing the sun or the solar goddess, Beaivi is very likely also present since she is the mother of humankind and all life on the Earth for traditional Sami people.

Rounding out a drum's decoration might be images of the landscape such as the conical nomadic dwellings called a *lávvu*, reindeer pens, various clan characters, and a *sieidi. Sieidi* were sacred places on the landscape, such as prominent outcrops of bedrock, large flat rocks, a single post, a cairn of pilled stones, or tree stumps recognized as portals into the spirit realm. Offerings were placed on these "doorsteps" to provide gifts to the spirits, thereby insuring a good hunt, good health, and protection against misfortune. These images are painted in a stylized manner that resembles the 8,000- to 10,000-year-old petroglyphs from the region. This chart lists a few examples of the images that can be found on a Sami shaman's *goavdi*. Actual drums can have many images, and some examples are decorated with nearly one hundred separate figures.

Figure 20. Sami *goavdi* collected in Folldalen, Nord Trøndelag, Norway in 1727. (Permanent collection of the Meininger Museum, Meiningen, Germany. Pen and ink © 2013 Evelyn C. Rysdyk)

Beaivi

The sun is honored as the goddess Beaivi who is the source of all life. This image is often positioned in the center of the drum face.

Maderáhkká

This is the Sami Earth Mother spirit.

The Moon

The *Lávvu*

Similar to a tepee, the *lávvu* is the traditional nomadic home for the Sami who follow the migrating reindeer.

The *Noaidi* (Shaman)

Here the Sami shaman is depicted with his *goavdi* (drum) in one hand and his drum "hammer" made from a reindeer antler in the other.

Heargi

The reindeer was as important to traditional Sami people as the bison was to Native Americans. Among many other uses, the reindeer was essential as source of food, leather for clothing, antlers for tools. The animals were also tamed and used for transportation.

Saaraahka

One of the three daughters of Maderáhkká, this spirit was a guardian over the female mysteries of fertility, menstruation, love, sexuality, pregnancy, and childbirth.

Sieidi

These landscape features were considered spirit portals that provided the Sami people with places to perform offerings to the spirits.

Flying Bird

This symbol has many similarities to bird and shaman figures from Siberia.

Hunter
Living as hunters, fishers, gatherers, and herders, the Sami's traditional lifestyle depended upon the spirits of nature for survival.

Reindeer Pen
The Sami herd was a combination of domesticated and wild reindeer.

The Sun
Another image of the goddess Beaivi.

As you can see, these figures are very simple ways to represent the elements of the Sami shaman's world, but your diagram of your spiritual realms and their inhabitants can be created in many ways. It can be drawn on deerskin with a pyrography iron, painted on a piece of wood, carved into the inner bark of a birch, embroidered on a piece of cloth, collaged from magazine photos, or made any other way that feels right. The idea is to create a representation of your spiritual realms and the beings that populate them. This assists in bridging the visible and invisible worlds and so supports you to feel the spirits' presence in your ordinary life. The following exercise will guide you through the steps of creating such an image to honor your spiritual connections.

Exercise: Making a Diagram of Your Spiritual World and Connections

Materials and Tools

- Something that you have chosen as a surface on which you will create your diagram. Pick a material that will suit your needs. For instance, if you need it to be portable, find something lightweight like leather, cloth, or paper. If you prefer something more permanent, your diagram could be created on a piece of plywood or stretched canvas that can be mounted on a wall or painted on the flat top of a small table. You may choose to paint on a drum or on the outside of a bag that holds your sacred objects. Take time to think about how you will display or use your diagram before you choose a surface.

- Pad of drawing paper as large as your finished diagram

- A mechanical pencil with 3H lead

- A good pair of scissors

- A way to make photocopies of your sketches

- A glue stick

- Graphite transfer paper (available at most craft stores) to transfer your diagram drawing to your final surface (It comes in white as well as gray if your final surface is a dark color.)

- Artist's archival masking tape that won't mar your finished surface or leave behind a sticky residue

- Paint, pyrography iron, colored pencils, embroidery floss, or other artist materials appropriate for your chosen surface to complete your finished diagram

Prepare for this process by journaling a list of all the sacred places in your Upper, Middle, and Lower Worlds. Now add your helping spirits, power animal, and guides. Add the places that make your home dear to you, your loved ones and companions. Include special animals, birds, plants, or natural forces you feel a heart connection with. It is also important to do a journey to ask your helping spirits what needs to be included and how your diagram will be used. Read through all the directions prior to starting work on your diagram.

Making Your Diagram

On the day you are ready to work on your diagram, prepare by doing an offering to the spirits to thank them for their help. Take time to pray and spiritually cleanse your self, your materials, and your space. You may use fragrant smoke from incense, sweetgrass, cedar, or sage for this or a spray of water to which perfume or unscented flower essences have been added to cleanse and sweeten the space. You may want to work accompanied by beautiful music or in sweet silence. Make your space as pleasant as possible to honor the sacredness of your work.

1. Using your pad of paper, create the individual sketches of your diagram's elements. Use reference photos or draw your elements freehand.

2. Once you have all of your elements sketched, cut them out, and then use a fresh sheet of paper to arrange them to your liking. You may want to place your most important spiritual connection in the center or make it larger than the rest. Use photocopies to reduce or enlarge each element until it feels right.

3. Once you are happy with the arrangement, paste the elements into place using the glue stick.

4. When your elements are all glued down, make a photocopy of the final drawing. Be sure it is the same size that you want your final diagram.

5. Cut out a piece of transfer paper at the exact same size as your final drawing.

6. Use the archival artist masking tape to *gently* attach the transfer paper to your final surface. Make sure that the side of the transfer paper with graphite is facing down, toward your surface. The "clean" side should be facing up.

7. Place your photocopied drawing on top of the transfer paper. Make sure it is positioned exactly as you want the finished diagram. Once you are happy with the placement, tape the photocopy on top of the graphite paper.

8. Make sure that the tape on the transfer paper and the tape on the photocopied drawing are tight and secure. If the tape is loose, and either one comes undone during the transfer process, it will be nearly impossible to get everything to line up properly again.

9. Start tracing every line of your drawing with the 3H pencil. Press hard enough to allow the graphite paper to transfer your drawing well. Make sure you trace all the details!

10. Once you have traced all the lines in your design, gently peel up one corner of your drawing and graphite paper to reveal your surface. Check to see that your tracing is strong and all the details have transferred.

11. If you are happy with the transfer, completely peel away the drawing and transfer paper.

12. You are now ready to use your art materials to create your finished diagram on your surface. This may be in paint, embroidery floss, pyrography, or whatever else you have chosen to use.

13. Your finished diagram can now be empowered by your helping spirits. If you are unsure about how to do this, do a journey to your helping spirits to ask them to aid you. Once the diagram is fully enlivened, make an offering to the spirits to thank them for their loving guidance and support in this process.

Journey Explorations

- Journey to a teacher or power animal to ask: "What are the ways I am to use this spirit diagram in my shamanic practice?" Record the content of your journey and your perceptions about what you receive.

- Now that your diagram has been empowered, it is a living being that requires special care. Journey to a teacher or power animal to ask: "What is the best way to care for my spiritual diagram's spirit?"

After each journey, make an offering of gratitude to all the spirits represented in your diagram.

Process Questions

- Write down in your journal what it was like to create a "map" or diagram of your spiritual world.

- How does this map relate to your ordinary reality?

Record your impressions in your journal.

CHAPTER 4

Creating a Shaman Tree

One of the ways that you can ground your spirit walker practice in your everyday life is to dedicate a special place in nature as a sacred space. Like the diagram in the previous chapter, this place provides an honored home for the spirits and gives the spirit walker a way to interact with them in this reality. One wonderful way to create such a place is to dedicate a shaman tree that will become your place for offerings, your gratitude prayers, and honoring the spirits in all the realms. I have such a tree in my suburban yard. However, even urban apartment dwellers can create this kind of sacred space on a balcony or in a corner of a room with a potted tree such as a fig tree or Norfolk Island pine. Another option is to work with your neighbors to dedicate a tree on your block or in the local green space to be a site for everyone to place gratitude prayers. This sort of practice is common across Siberia and central Asia, where people have dedicated trees to be special places on the landscape that become the focus for entire communities to pray and make offerings.

Your tree may be located in a prominent place near a mountain, at a crossroads, on the site of a spring, on a riverbank, in a clearing in a forest, or any location where there is a strong sense of the spirits of the land. These spirits, referred to as *Cher Ezed* in the Tuvan language, are thought of as masters or owners of these places. The shamans negotiate with these owners, or *ezed*, so that their people and the livestock under their care are able to thrive. To ensure that the spirits of nature feel treasured and honored, the Tuvan people dedicate particular trees as places through which the *ezed* of nature may be honored.

Figure 21. Dedicated shaman tree in the author's yard. (Author's photo)

Depending upon the local customs, these specially honored trees may be a pine, a birch, or a larch. The tree is chosen for being especially tall, very ancient, and/or having a special shape, unusual branches, or an auspicious number of trunks. Trees with three trunks are thought of as money or abundance trees in Tuva, whereas a tree with two trunks might be dedicated to honor a marriage or the union of two clans. Trees with nine trunks, which started life as a small cluster of saplings sprouted from one root, are especially sacred across the region as nine is considered the most sacred number in Tuvan culture.

They honor nine sacred springs, nine sacred mountains, and nine sacred celestial objects; the sun, the moon, and the seven stars of the "Great Bear" or Big Dipper.

Other times, a tree is chosen simply due to its proximity to a place that is to be honored, such as a sacred spring or waterfall. In this case, the tree may be of any species.

Once a tree is chosen, the shaman performs a special blessing ritual to sanctify the tree as a place for ritual. This blessing dedicates the tree as a place where prayers may be carried directly into the spirit worlds. This is possible as all trees are echoes of the great World Tree that unites all the realms of the spirits and connects the heavens to the Earth. In addition, offerings made at this special shaman tree strengthen the spirits of place and support the fertility of the land and livestock, as well as encourage harmony, luck, and good health for the people. Here is a prayer from the Tuva that communicates the sense of how important the spirits of place are to the welfare of all beings:

> *From the ezed of the mountains that stand imposingly,*
> *From the ezed of water that rushes noisily,*
> *From the ezed of mountains that are many-peaked,*
> *From the ezed of grasses and trees that grow*
> *multibranched,*
> *We beg good fortune.*
> *From the ezed of flowing waters,*
>   *the ezed of whirlpools at river bends,*
>   *the ezed of airy winds,*
>   *the ezed of lying stones,*
> *We beg good fortune.*[6]

When the late Tuvan shaman Ai Churek facilitated a shaman tree ceremony (known in the Tuvan language as an *Yyash Dagyyr*) for our students in 2004, she demonstrated how a tree is dedicated by first journeying to the spirits of the land. Since the strength of a tree depends upon having its roots deeply in the earth, it is important to honor the land spirits first and to ask permission for the ceremony. Then the area beneath the tree is prepared by clearing brush and grasses away so that it is possible to walk all the way around the tree. The tree and the area around its base are then fed with sprinkled milk in an offering ceremony.[7] The milk is tossed toward the tree, onto the ground, and up into the air. A Tuvan shaman would use a special nine-eyed wooden throwing spoon (*tos-karak* in the Tuvan language) for this purpose, but any spoon dedicated to sacred work can be used.

Figure 22. The author supporting her mother Agnes Rysdyk as Ai Churek braids the master *chalama* during a shaman tree dedication in 2004. (Photo: Carl A. Hyatt)

Next, four or more yards of cotton cloth in three solid colors—red, yellow, and blue—are braided into a master *chalama*, or prayer ribbon, that is tied around the trunk of the tree. If the tree happens to be especially large, nine yards would be used. While the shaman braids the fabric, the other end is held firmly by the oldest member of the community. This person is usually kneeling on the ground, but if that isn't possible, she or he may be seated on a sacred cloth. The elder person's role is as an anchor representing the spirits of the ancestors being "woven" into the *chalama* to reflect their ongoing connections to our world and to access their blessings for the tree and the community.

When the braiding of the fabric is completed, the cloth is tied around the trunk of the tree about four to five feet up from the ground. It is tied snuggly enough to keep it in place but not so tight as to choke the tree. The *chalama* must be long enough to leave "tails," after it is knotted. These may be anywhere from one foot to about three feet long. This master *chalama* braid will become the vessel that holds the smaller *chalama* that people leave as offerings to ask for blessings and to honor the spirits.

Once the master braid is in place, the shaman again blesses the tree by dancing and singing around it while drumming or rattling. The shaman's song, or *algysh* in Tuvan, is sung to praise the tree and its place in the Center of the Universe as a representative of the World Tree. Here is a translation of a typical *algysh* for the shaman tree:

> *Shaman tree, you are the most wonderful tree on the*
>   *Earth;*
> *Shaman tree, they say you are the most beautiful tree*
>   *in the world;*
> *Shaman tree, they say you are the goodness of an animal;*
> *Shaman tree, you embody all the spirits;*
> *Shaman tree, they say all the people's lives are tied*
>   *together in you;*
> *Shaman tree, they say you preserve among your*
>   *beautiful branches people's fortunes;*
> *Shaman tree! They say you give your healthfulness to*
>   *the animals;*
> *Shaman tree! They say you give children a happy life;*
> *Shaman tree, sacred tree.*[8]

At this point, the *chalama* and the tree would again be fed with milk and small pinches of cooked rice. Women go around the tree nine times and men go around the tree three times as they make their offerings. These offerings are extended with gratitude for the blessings the spirits provide. As it is with other indigenous cultures around the world, the offerings not only give thanks for what already is in place in our lives, but in advance for the blessings to come.

Once trees are dedicated in this fashion, the subsequent offerings at these trees would include tying smaller braids or strips of cloth to the master *chalama*. In Mongolia, the dominant color used for such offerings is a sky-colored, brilliant blue that may be either cotton or silk. These cloth offerings are threaded into the braided fabric of the master *chalama* and securely tied. If there are low branches, the smaller *chalama* or strips of cloth may be attached to the tree's branches. When tied directly to the tree, these cloth offerings are only half knotted and never secured too tightly so as not to choke the growth of the sacred tree. Other typical offerings include milk, clear alcohol such as vodka, cooked rice, and sometimes sweets. Whichever form of offering is used, the person making the offering always walks around the tree three times clockwise while chanting and praying thanks to the spirits.

Where there are no trees, the people of central Asia pile rocks to create an artificial mound. This conical rock cairn, known alternately as an *ovaa* (*ovoo* in Mongolian), may be a small pile no higher than the knees or as large as a small hill. Sometimes, a sapling or wooden pole is erected in its center to function in the same fashion as the shaman tree. The Tuvan ceremony to dedicate such a place is called an *Ovaa Dagyyr*. When a pile of stones is used as the sacred location, it is typical to leave an offering of a stone as well as a fabric tie. By bringing a stone, the person adds to the size and therefore the power of the sacred place. As with the tree, the *ovaa* is circumnavigated three times by the person as they pray their gratitude to the spirits.

Exercise: Dedicating the Shaman Tree

As you have done with each exercise in this book, read through this chapter and instructions thoroughly before you begin.

Materials and Tools

- Your rattle

- Several large, grapefruit- or melon-sized stones

- A stick of butter

- Four yards of solid red cotton cloth (approximately twenty inches wide)

- Four yards of solid yellow cotton cloth (approximately twenty inches wide)

- Four yards of solid blue cotton cloth (approximately twenty inches wide)

- Three small spools of half-inch ribbon in solid colors, such as red, yellow, and blue, or blue, green, and purple, or red, yellow, and orange

- A spoon

- A small bowl of milk

- A small bowl of cooked rice

- Your other offering materials

Choosing the Tree

1. First, journey with your power animal or teacher to meet the spirits of your land. Ask the spirits to show you which

tree would be the best "candidate" for your shaman tree. Also ask the spirits of the land how they would like to be honored as a part of the ceremony you will be performing.

2. Once the tree has been chosen, honor the spirits of the directions by shaking your rattle[9] and merge with your power animal and sing your power song. While merged and in a prayerful state, do the work of clearing away brush and grass at the base of the tree so that it is easier to walk around. Do this work with a loving attitude as you are creating sacred space. As you complete this phase, make offerings to the tree and the land with pinches of cooked rice in gratitude for their willingness to participate in the ceremony.

3. Place the rocks in a circle around the base of the tree and bless them with butter. As you work, sing to the other beneficial spirits of the land and let them know that you wish them to find good and comfortable homes amid these stones.

Braiding the Master *Chalama*

The master *chalama* is braided from the three colors of cloth. Since it is quite a bit of fabric, have someone, preferably an elder, hold the other ends of the cloth as you braid them. If you are working alone, secure the ends of the fabric to a nail or weigh it down securely so that you will find it easier to braid. Sing your power song as you braid the cloth so that you are empowering it as you work.

When it has been completed, tie the master *chalama* around the trunk of the tree. If the tree is one with multiple trunks, tie the *chalama* so that it enfolds all of them.

Feeding Brings it to Life

You are now ready to feed the *chalama*, fully bringing it and the tree to life as a sacred place. Sprinkle spoonfuls of milk on the *chalama*, on the tree, on the ground around the tree, and into the air. Thank all the spirits for gathering in this place and for listening to your prayers. Sing a song from your heart to give thanks. You may choose to use the Tuvan song lyrics or similar words. Remember, it is your grateful attitude that is the power behind whatever words you use.

Figure 23. Tuvan shaman feeding the site of a shaman tree with milk tossed from a *tos-karak* or nine-eyed offering spoon. (Pen and ink © 2013 Evelyn C. Rysdyk)

Making Offerings with the Wind

Since the tree is now activated, you may add individual prayer braids, or *chalamas*, made from the three colors of ribbon. These prayer braids can be offered for any purpose that is close to your heart. Give thanks for health, good friends, loving family, a roof over your head, and whatever else you feel enriches or blesses your life. You may also place gratitude prayers for what you are in the process of manifesting. Remember to feel that your prayer has already been fulfilled, so that you contribute to creating the reality for its manifestation. Close your ceremony with a heartfelt prayer of thanks to the spirits, to the land, and to your ancestors.

The wind will play with your cloth and ribbon offerings and contribute to sending the prayers that they represent throughout the realms and into all directions. As you add to this tree, you will find that it and its many braided expressions of gratitude connect you to everything in your life. The sacred tree becomes the center of your universe and a direct line to all the spirits.

Journey Explorations

- Journey with your power animal or teacher to meet with the spirit of the tree you have chosen to be your shaman prayer tree. Ask what your special tree would like in return for its gifts to you.

- Journey to a teacher or power animal to ask: "At what times is it appropriate for me to use my shaman tree?"

Record the content of each journey and your perceptions about what you receive.

Process Questions

- Write down in your journal what it was like to create a special place for your prayers.

- How does it feel to have this special tree support your process? Record your impressions.

- Articulate, as best as you can, in your journal, the bodily, emotional, and spiritual sensations you receive while working with the shaman tree.

- How can making prayers at your tree help you when you are feeling low or when you feel as though you need more support from the spirits?

Record all that you learn and make offerings in nature after each of the journeys.

CHAPTER 5

The Drum

The drum is the single object most strongly associated with the shaman. While these instruments also vary tremendously from one region and indeed from one practitioner to the next, they have many common traits. Drumming not only accompanies a shaman's journey to the spirit world, it alters the spirit walker's brain and body, as well. Sandra Harner, PhD, health research director for the Foundation for Shamanic Studies, has done work in determining the specific psychological and physiological effects of drumming and the shamanic journey process. Specifically, her experiments were focused on the effects drumming and shamanic journeying produced in the immune system among her test subjects.[10] In her research, Harner studied the drumming rhythm of four-beats-per-second, which is a rhythm commonly used to attain shamanic consciousness. In the presence of this rhythm, the brain becomes synchronized with the drumming. A listener's brain wave patterns change to match the four-cycle-per-second pulses of the theta brain wave state. This state supports the rich visual and auditory imagery typical of the shamanic journey experience.

Harner has concluded that shamanic journeying with drumming has measurable psychological effects producing increased affective, cognitive, physical, and total well-being—as tracked using tools such as the Schlosser Well-Being Scale, the State-Trait Anxiety Inventory, STAI form Y-2, the Short Imaginal Processes Inventory, and other metrics. In addition, as a part of this research, Harner collected specimens of saliva to measure the changes in salivary Immunoglobulin A (SIgA). This antibody, which is also found in blood, skin, and the gut, is one of the agents the human body uses to guard against infections by bacteria, viruses, and fungi. Specifically, the SIgA's role is in fighting respiratory and digestive infections. In her research, Harner observed that participants showed a rise in SIgA after shamanically journeying to the drum for a sustained period. In fact, test subjects who were surveyed again after a year showed much lower rates of colds and upper respiratory infections even though they were never told of the role SIgA plays in the human immune system.[11]

In her 2002 presentation at the Institute of Noetic Science, "Exploring the Frontiers of Consciousness" lecture series, Harner also observed that drumming itself—particularly in the range of four-beats-per-second—produced the effect of calming anxiety and relieving depression and tension among her subjects. She postulates that because drumming is a sound comprised of many low frequencies and high amplitudes, it has a greater effect over a larger area of the brain than other sounds.[12] It seems that, basically, drumming has the effect of temporarily jamming the brain's circuits and, in that state, we find that our minds and bodies naturally gravitate toward feelings of harmony, well-being, and health. This is certainly a remarkable finding, but it may also help to partially explain the sheer staying power shamanism and the shamanic journey have had over the length and breadth of human culture.

Drums Worldwide

Drums are found in various forms around the globe. A type of drum widely used by the shamans of many cultures is the hoop or frame drum. The foundations of these drums are generally wood although some are made of materials as unusual as forged iron. In circumstances where wood is used, the hoop is created from a flat slat of wood bent into a hoop and secured. The shaping of the frame is accomplished either by using steam or boiling to soften the wood prior to its being bent or by bending the wood when it is still green. Once dry or seasoned, the hoop may be sanded or otherwise prepared to receive a drumhead, most commonly cut from animal skin. To prepare an animal skin for such a purpose, it must be removed carefully from the animal, scraped of extra flesh, washed in clean water, stretched and dried but not tanned, as is the case when hides are used to make leather. This cleaned and dried animal skin is referred to as rawhide. When the rawhide is ready to be used in the making of a drum, it is soaked again in water to re-soften it. The hide is then stretched across the drum frame and secured. This method results in a membrane that will, when dry, vibrate when struck with either the hand or a drumbeater. This is a simple and time-tested formula for creating a drum; however, it can result in a remarkable range of unique variations.

For instance, among the peoples of Siberia, each tribal culture has its own variation on the frame drum theme. The drum was considered so sacred among these tribes that they would substitute metaphoric phrases when referring to the instrument rather than using its actual name. This same tradition is followed when addressing or referring to their most esteemed spirits such as the Bear. Among the Nenets and Enets for instance, the drum is referred to variously as "the larch bow," "the sky bow," and "the curved tree" among other names.[13] These names refer both to the material of the hoop—wood from the larch tree which is sacred to many of the Siberian tribes—as well as the use of the drum, that is, as a device which shoots the shaman off into the spirit realms. These drums are usually sixteen to eighteen inches in diameter and about three to four inches deep.

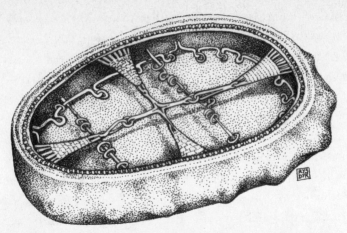

Figure 24. This drawing illustrates the iron wire and ring-shaped jingles that were an integral part of an Evenk shaman's drum. The cross-shaped hand piece is connected to the drum frame with woven leather straps. This cross is pierced in the center to represent the shaman's entrance into the spirit realms. The edge of the reindeer hide has been decorated with colored beads. (Pen and ink ©2013 Evelyn C, Rysdyk—from an exhibition photograph. Illinois State Museum/Russian Museum of Ethnography)

The Enets drum is a hoop of larch wood usually covered with deer rawhide. Among the Siberian peoples, a shaman may be either male or female. Any drum being made for a female Enets shaman would be covered with the skin from a healthy doe, whereas for a male shaman a skin from a buck was used for the drumhead. The animals from which these hides were taken were chosen for their strength and grace. No weakened or old animals were ever used in the making of a ritual drum.[14]

On the Nenets and Enets drum, there are a series of lugs or wide pins inserted around the frame over which the hide is stretched. This produces a look of bumps around the drum's circumference. Drums of the Nganasan people, who live to the east of the Enets on the Taymyr Peninsula in the Russian Arctic, are created in a similar style. Examples seen on a 1978 Russian Academy of Sciences expedition were approximately twenty inches across and seven to eight inches deep.[15] These lugs are used to tighten the drumhead when the hide becomes loose from either extended use or humidity. The Nenets and Enets used pegs of larch wood for this purpose; however, among shamans of particularly high and powerful status—known as *vydutana* (Nenets) or *budtode* (Enets)—bear teeth were substituted for the wooden pegs.

On the back of the drum some kind of handle is fashioned so that the shaman may comfortably hold it while she or he works with the spirits. On an Enets drum, this is a crosspiece fashioned of iron wire. For the Nenets and some other tribes, the crosspiece is made of wood. These wooden handles are shaped to fit the hand, and sometimes also carved to resemble a figure. On the inside of the drum, along these crosspieces, objects of ritual significance are often hung. These can include fetish-type carvings of the shaman's spirit helpers, strips of cloth, feathers, and iron jingles or bells.

Figure 25. A Yukaghir shaman's drum. The bumps around the circumference of the drum frame help to hold the hide away from the hoop and so allow more resonance. (Pen and ink ©2013 Evelyn C. Rysdyk)

The Yukaghir people, who live in the northeastern area of Siberia, near to the Even and Evenk people, also used very large lug-framed drums often more oval in shape. The Yukaghir word for drum is *yalgil*, which means lake. This refers to the spirit lake in which the shaman must dive to enter the spirit world.[16] This makes sense since, based on their language, the Yukaghir originate from a Paleo-Asiatic people who originally lived near Lake Baikal.[17] Some of these large drums are over a yard long and nearly two feet wide![18]

These larger drums are seen in early 20th-century ethnographic photographs of people from farther south in Siberia as well. For instance, the Karagass people, who live on the northern slopes of the Sayan Mountains in conical tents resembling those of the Sami, northern Evenks, Nganasan, and other reindeer herders, have drums that resemble those of the Nenets and Enets, but on a larger scale. Examples of drums over twenty-four inches across and approximately eight inches deep are found among these people.[19] Presumably, based on the people's cultural livelihood, the heads of these drums were also made of reindeer skin. Perhaps because these tribal groups have similar livelihoods and rely on the same resources, there are some overall similarities in their worldviews. This may explain the converging structures of their ritual implements.

Other designs of frame drums are seen among Siberian peoples as well. The shamans of Tuva use large frame drums, as do the Buryat shamans. These drums have long, colorful, cloth streamers attached to their frames that produce marvelous, birdlike flutters when the shamans dance. This use of cloth strips or streamers to decorate a shaman's drum is commonly seen in southern Siberia across the Asian steppes and into China. Depending on the region, similar streamers or fringes are attached to the shaman's coat sleeves and hem as well so that an overall flying effect is produced when the shaman dances while journeying. Indeed, Siberian shamans were said to "cross the boundaries of time and space to change their essence and appearance [into that of animals or birds] and it is this idea that is reflected by the symbolism of the shaman's coat."[20]

Some tribes use drum handles that are flexible. The Buryat, for instance, use a cross brace of leather cord across the back of the drum. This allows the frame to be shaken easily so that the bells attached around the drum frame's outer circumference may be jingled as the shaman works. The Ulchi people of the lower Amur River basin of Siberia exploit the strategy of using a flexible back to its finest extreme. Their drums have fairly large frames, approximately twenty-four inches in diameter and quite shallow at only about two inches deep. The flexible leather handles offer the ability to create several different sounds during the shaman's journey. By shaking the drum, the shaman is able to produce a tone whereby the rear of the drumhead strikes the knuckles of the hand holding the back straps. In addition, a beater is used to strike the face of the drum in the traditional manner, and the rim may be hit to produce yet another separate tone. The effects that are possible using these three different tones are quite elaborate. In fact, an Ulchi shaman produces different rhythm patterns with these three drum tones for each individual spirit encountered on a shamanic journey. While working with the spirits, the journeying shaman sings, dances, and simultaneously beats out complex patterns on the drum. It's quite a remarkable feat, especially when you realize that the shaman performs while in trance!

The Ulchi drumbeater is long, flat, and somewhat paddle-shaped in appearance with a short handle. The flat head of the beater is wrapped in fur. This *geespu* may be used by the shaman as a tool for healing as well as a drumbeater. At the end of a *kamlanie*, or spiritual healing ceremony, the shaman sometimes places the *geespu* on the patient's head to fasten or seal a healing into the patient's body.

Figure 26. Grandfather Misha playing a Ulchi drum with his flat *geespu*. The drum handle has flexible straps. (Pen and ink ©2013 Evelyn C, Rysdyk)

It is worth noting here that a common belief among shamanic cultures is that virtually all of the shaman's paraphernalia and ritual apparel may be imbued with spiritual energy. In other words, just as the shaman can merge with his or her power animal or teacher's spirit, so too may each healing tool become enlivened with spirits. In this paradigm, the shaman's drum, drumbeater, rattle, and costume work in partnership with the shaman. It is also believed that these living objects have the capacity to operate independently. In essence, they have the ability to act as healers themselves. For instance, a drumbeater may be placed on one part of a patient to affect a healing while the shaman herself works directly on another part of the person. In addition, the shaman may use an empowered drum, beater, or other object to work on multiple patients. Even though the shaman may have only touched one person, the other people are said to receive benefits since the healing spirits that actually do the work were operating through both the empowered objects and the shaman him or herself.

Other peoples around the globe use different sorts of frame drums. Among the people of the North American Arctic, frame drums are fairly large but most often quite shallow at only about an inch or so in depth and therefore quite light-weight. Alutiiq drums, or *cauyaq*, have a narrow oval hoop over which a polar bear lung sack or halibut stomach is stretched and secured. In Greenland, the drum, or *qilaat*, is made from an oval wooden frame covered with the bladder of a polar bear. Like the drums of the Yup'ik and Inupiaq people, these have a handle at the bottom of their rim. This gives them an appearance rather like very large lollipops on very short sticks. These drums have very narrow frames and are usually played by hitting the frame with a thin stick, instead of the skin itself. The hide-covered drums may be easily twirled or rotated by the handles during the shaman's dance. On some examples from this area, the handles are carved to resemble human figures.[21] Sometimes, these figures bear the signs of a shaman's initiatory experience of being dismembered by the spirits. Like the spirit figures called *saivens* of the Ulchi that bear illness or wounds for the people, these types of handles act as a stand-in or representation of the shaman, functioning as proof that the person bearing it is a shaman and therefore has a right to enter into the spirit world. It was thought that this identification badge would keep the shaman safe from spiritual harm while doing battle with the spirits of illness.

The Chukchee people of far eastern Siberia share some cultural similarities with the people of Arctic North America. Their drums are covered in a skin made from a walrus's stomach and also have a handle like Inuit drums. They are quite lightweight, at only about a pound to a pound and a half and are about sixteen to eighteen inches across.[22] People of the Pacific Northwest region of North America use single-sided frame drums for their dances and ceremonies. These drums have either leather cords or wooden handles on the back. Drums that were used for shamanic purposes, however, would differ from the other drums by the addition of painted images on the inside of the drumhead. These paintings were either clan association images or the shaman's guardian spirits. In addition to the frame drum, Tlingit tribal shamans also used a box-shaped drum. These drums were constructed like wooden chests and were beaten on top with either the hands or a drumstick. Only a few, incomplete examples of these drums remain in museum collections.[23]

An interesting variation on the frame-handled drum may be seen among the people of Inner Mongolia. In this culture, drums are most often covered in pigskin; however, it is the frame that is most interesting and sets these drums apart. It is constructed from a ring of wrought iron forged with a handle that ends at the bottom in a series of loops. Each of these loops has, suspended from it, several smaller iron rings. These iron rings function as jingles that accompany the rhythms beaten out on the drum while the shaman dances.[24]

Figure 27. Inner Mongolian shaman's drum. This drum has a forged iron frame, iron jingles, and a rawhide drumhead. (Pen and ink © 2013 Evelyn C. Rysdyk)

Living near the Mongol people are the Manchu. Most Manchu-style drums are small, wood-framed hoop drums that have pigskin hides secured with brass tacks along the hoop's outer edge. The most unusual feature of these drums is the series of Chinese coins and flattened, pierced bottle caps strung along a wire secured in a horizontal line across the top of the drum's back. Twisting the drum while it is being beaten causes the coins to slide back and forth along the wire creating a musical jingle. This sound is accomplished by rotating the wrist that holds the drum very rapidly. This second sound is combined with drumming to produce the patterned rhythms a shaman wishes to play.

Figure 28. Nepalese *jhankri* (shaman) Bhola Nath Banstola holding his *dhyangro* drum. (Author's photo)

Himalayan shamanic drums, known as *dhyangro*, have deep frames and are held by a handle attached to the rim. This handle ends in the form of the *phurba*, or three-sided ritual dagger, used by the *jhankri*, or shaman. The drum itself has a male skin on one side and a female skin on the other, determined not by the gender of the animal source of the hide, but rather by the relationship to the handle's three-sided blade that will be discussed further in chapter 14. Thanks to its unique handle, the *dhyangro* may be spun back and forth to either side while it is being played. Inside the drum are charms, sacred beads, or stones to enliven the instrument and to rattle as it is spun. The Nepalese drumbeater is piece of supple wood or bamboo that has been bent and dried into a bow shape allowing the shaman to beat the drum skin that is facing away from him or her. In this way the sound of the drumbeats are directed into the shaman's body.

Figure 29. A Nepalese *dhyangro* with bent willow beater. (Pen and ink © 2013 Evelyn C. Rysdyk)

The Sami people of Arctic Scandinavia and the Kola Peninsula of Russia use both frame drums and an unusual type of bowl drum, all of which tend to be more oval-shaped than round. Sami frame drums are made in three different varieties: the curved hoop drum, or *gievre*, made from one or two strips of thin pine or birch bent and secured with sinew; the ring drum, which is also known as a *gievre* although it is created from a thin slice of the circumference of a large pine tree; and the *kannus*, which is made from a length of wood that has been notched so that it can be bent round. Because of its more rugged construction, the *kannus* is the largest of the Sami drum styles.[25]

Figure 30. Sami drum with twisted leather fringe and brass jingles attached to the rim. Norsk Folkemuseum, collected Nordland, Bindal, 1925. (Pen and ink ©2013 Evelyn C. Rysdyk from a photo in the European Digital Library: european.eu.)

The *gievre*-style of Sami drums is largely found among the southern Sami people, and the *kannus* is used by the Kemi Sami of northern Finland. The curved hoop-style of *gievre* has its reindeer hide head secured around the circumference of the drum with wooden pegs. When it is viewed from the front, the drum appears rather like a sun with radiating rays. Both the *gievre* and *kannus* have vertical wooden handles on the back and usually an additional cross brace of either wood or leather to which sacred objects such as bear teeth, bones, small brass rings, and copper or silver amulets are tied. This echoes the Siberian custom of tying sacred objects and jingles to the drum.

The more unusual bowl drum, or *goavdi*, of the northern Sami, is created from a nodule of pine, spruce, or curly birch. Curly birch is wood from a birch tree that has been attacked by a parasite that causes the grain of the wood to grown in beautiful, chaotic whorls. The nodule is cut from the tree and then hollowed out into a bowl, after which two long, parallel holes are cut from the bottom to create a natural handle. These holes also allow the drum maker to get his or her hands inside the drum to secure the reindeer hide to the edge of the drum. Other holes may also be cut into the bowl to increase the volume of the drum as well as reduce the overall weight of the bowl's frame. A series of small holes are drilled just in from the edge of the bowl for sewing the drumhead to the frame.

Other kinds of drums, such as cylindrical or tube-shaped drums are as widely spread over the globe as frame drums. Most often these are made from sections of tree trunks that have been hollowed out either by natural means or by the drum maker. They may have heads at either one or two ends and are played while they sit on the ground, are held under the arm, or rest over the knee of the player. If they are played on the ground, they may either be placed on their rim or on end, depending on the style of drum. Cylindrical drums are widely seen among African tribes, Native American peoples, and the people of the Amazon.

The Spirit Walker's Drum

Contemporary spirit walkers may also augment their "shamanic tool kit" with the addition of a drum with a synthetic or Mylar head. While not as beautiful as a well-made drum of wood and hide, these drums offer the practicality of being dimensionally stable in any weather. The drumhead will neither stretch nor shrink with changes in temperature and humidity. They are also much more resistant to the bumps and bangs typical when traveling with your drum and the hazards of airplane luggage compartments. This kind of drum is therefore especially useful when a shamanic practitioner is called to move extensively from place to place or needs to work outdoors in damp weather.

If you are interested in buying a drum, find a drum shop or local drum maker that will allow you to try them before your buy. Play each one to see what feels right in your hand, looks pleasing to your eyes, sounds best to your ears, and connects with your heart. Every drum has a different voice and feel. Experiment with different sizes, different drumheads or hides, and different beaters until you are satisfied that you have the right combination. If you are fortunate to be purchasing a drum from a local craftsperson, ask about the materials and how they were prepared. Some drum makers create their drums in ceremony and are willing to share the intent they had in making the drum. Whatever drum you choose will become a partner in your spirit walker practice, so take the time to really know what you are getting.

Exercise: Making a Rawhide Frame Drum

Although at last count I have more than a dozen personal drums, the ones I have made myself hold the most power for me. When I first began my shamanic practice years ago, I made my first drum and enjoyed the process so much that I constructed many others. Some of these I eventually sold to my shamanic colleagues. While the process is messy and sometimes a bit frustrating, the result will be a drum that you can truly call your own.

Unlike in the early days of my own drum-making adventures, there are now several companies that provide easy-to-follow frame drum kits. Two I have used are Cedar Mountain Drums (*www.cedarmtndrums.com*) and Centralia Fur and Hide (*https://furandhide.com*). When choosing a kit, make sure you select a drum in the fourteen to eighteen inch range. Drums that are smaller than fourteen inches in diameter often sound weak or too high, while drums larger than eighteen inches in diameter are too heavy for a person of average height to comfortably hold. A good way to judge what size will work for you is to measure your own body. With your arm bent to ninety degrees at the elbow, use a yardstick to measure the distance from the inside of the crook of your elbow to the tip of your middle finger. The result should be the approximate drum diameter that will work best for you.

Drum kits may have either round or octagonal hoops and may offer a selection of different kinds of woods such as maple, oak, or cedar. The kits may also offer a choice for the kind of animal hide that will become the drum's face. Typical options are deer or elk hide; however, sometimes it is possible to get kits with horse, bison, moose, bear, or other kinds of rawhide as well. If you are unsure about what kind of hoop or hide you should get, by all means journey to your spirit teacher or power animal. It is also a really good idea to talk to the company that is providing the kit. They may have recommendations for the beginning drum maker that will make your process go more smoothly. While some companies include a drumbeater with each kit, it is important to make sure you purchase a drumbeater or beater kit when you order your drum kit.

When your kit arrives, read through the instructions to get an idea of what sort of preparations are necessary—such as presoaking the rawhide the night prior to making your drum. On the day you are ready to actually make your drum, gather all the materials suggested in the instructions.

When you are ready to begin the process, prepare yourself and the space in which you are working with a prayer of gratitude. Remember, the elements of your sacred drum began as a living animal and a tree. As such, they deserve your gratitude and loving respect. Also honor the spirits that you work with such as your power animal and teacher as you create sacred space by honoring the directions. You may also want to make an offering outside to thank the spirits in advance for their help. Once you have spiritually set the stage for your work, follow the instructions that are included with your kit.

When you have finished making your drum, leave it in a warm, dry place (that is, away from heat sources) and allow it to dry completely. Your drum's voice will only become apparent when the drum is totally dry. The rawhide will become stiff again and vibrate fully when beaten. Having completed your drum, give another prayer of gratitude for all that you have learned in the process, and then go outside to make another offering.

I have also written some instructions that may be downloaded if you want to try tackling drum making without a kit at *www.myspiritwalk.com*. While more challenging than working from a kit, I find creating a drum "from scratch" a remarkably rewarding and fulfilling experience.

Exercise: Journeying to Empower Your Drum

A drum is just a musical instrument until the spirit walker empowers it for a sacred purpose. Whether you have made your drum or chosen one that was made by someone else, you will need to empower it.

When you are ready to dedicate your drum to your shamanic practice, make a gratitude offering to the spirits. Honor that which you have been given and your connections to the world of spiritual power. Also remember to thank the spirits of the tree and animal of which your drum is made. They are no longer in physical form and must be honored for the lives they have given for your drum.

1. Call with your heart to bring your power animal to you.

2. When you feel ready, merge with your animal and begin to sing your power song while holding the drum in a loving embrace.

3. After a while, begin beating the drum with the journey rhythm. Close your eyes and allow the drum to carry you into the spirit world to the spirit of your Upper World teacher.

4. Ask the spirit teacher to merge with your drum. You may feel the drum get warm, or you may feel it become heavier or lighter.

5. As a part of the ceremony of empowering, you may be called on to participate by breathing on the hide, singing, or dancing with the drum. Allow the guidance from your spirit teacher to lead you.

6. When the process is complete, beat the rhythm of the callback, unmerge, and return yourself to ordinary reality.

Upon your return at the callback signal, take ample time to sit with the experience prior to recording it in your notebook. Remember to go outside and make an offering of thanks. Let your heart fill with gratitude for the gifts you have received in this experience and place an offering on the Earth with reverence.

Caring for Your Drum

A rawhide drum is somewhat of a living, breathing thing even before it is empowered, due to the nature of the skin used for its face. As such, a drum needs to be treated like a baby or beloved pet. For instance, don't leave your drum in the sun or a hot car—the skin will quickly shrink to the point of tearing. Your drum is also subject to climatic conditions. The hide will stretch and contract with changes in humidity. As much as is possible, store your drum in a dry place with even temperature.

In damp, humid, or cold conditions, you may find that your rawhide drum absorbs moisture from the air, which causes the head to loosen. This gives the drum a deadened, dull sound. One solution for this problem is to slowly warm the drum in front a fire or heater or to use a hair dryer to take out some of the moisture. Take care not to overheat the drum and do not hold it too close to a heat source, especially if using a heater or fire. Stay present with the drum as it dries. Do not simply leave the drum near the heat source and walk away, as the drum could easily overtighten and tear if you aren't keeping an eye on its progress. I have found that gently heating the drum from the back using a hair dryer works quite well.

The kind of reusable dehumidifier tins filled with silica gel employed by woodworkers and gunsmiths can be helpful as well. They are slim perforated tin boxes holding crystals that absorb excess moisture. They usually have an indicator that lets you know when they are depleted, and they can be easily restored to use by heating in an oven. These kinds of dehumidifiers work best if you store your drum in an airtight case or bag. Placing your drum and the reusable dehumidifier inside a large plastic bag and then inside of your normal drum case will help to make it more airtight.

If, on the other hand, you live in a hot dry climate or use central heating during the winter months, your drum may get too dry and become overly tight. This will make the sound too high and, if left alone, may also do irreparable damage causing the drum's head to split or tear. A temporary solution for this problem is to mist some water into the back of the drum with a spray bottle. Rub the water into the rawhide with your hand so it is absorbed. This act will balance out the moisture content in the hide. Don't use too much water on your drum as it may develop a wavy surface and the tone will go flat.

I have found that treating the hide of my drum with animal fat and wax protects the hide from the overdry conditions of our winter's arid heating season as well as during the humid months of our Maine coastal summers. Different drum makers have different drum dressing formulas that they find work best. Nearly all of them include an animal fat and some also have some beeswax or oil included in the mix. In all cases, the treatment is worked into the hide with bare hands. Some folks use pure lanolin. Thanks to a dear Penobscot native friend of mine, I use rendered bear fat to treat my drum hides. Nicholas Wood, the publisher of *Sacred Hoop* magazine and a very talented shamanic crafter from the UK, recommends using "dubbin," which is a treatment for leather shoes and boots. Typically, dubbin is a mixture of natural wax (such as beeswax) oil and tallow, another rendered animal fat, or lanolin. This kind of product is sold by shoe manufacturers, like Dr. Martens (Wonder Balsam) or in places that sell horse tack and saddles. Since you will be rubbing this into your hide by hand, always make sure that whatever you use is safe to handle.

A special note here: If you have plans to paint your drum, make sure to do it *before* using dressing! Otherwise, the greases in the dressing will make it impossible for paints to adhere to the surface of the rawhide. If you have treated the surface and then decide to paint your drum, use a cloth moistened with artist-quality odorless mineral spirits to remove the hide dressing before painting.

Know that all of these products will change the appearance of the hide slightly—making it a touch darker and more honey-colored. If that is concerning, use a bit of the dressing on the back of the hide first as a test. If you are happy with the look, work the dressing into the hide on the front and back. Start with a small amount of dressing, as it is very hard to take it off if you overdo it. Work it into the hide until it soaks in. Once you are finished, allow it to sit for a day, then buff off any excess dressing with a dry, soft cloth.

Finally, remember your sacred drum began its life as an animal and a tree. As such, it is important to always treat it with loving respect!

Decorating Your Drum

Once you have empowered your drum, you may want to decorate it to further personalize it. If you find that you are drawn

Figure 31. Variations on the frame drum theme. Left is an Ulchi drum with flexible straps, center is a Sami-style bowl drum with a reindeer antler beater and right is a drum with a Siberian-style, effigy handle. (Author's photo)

to paint the drum face with a design, use a high-quality artist acrylic paint. (Note: If you have applied dressing to the raw-hide, the paint will not adhere. You will have to clean the drum face with a soft cloth and a small amount of artist-quality odorless mineral spirits first.) You can sketch out your design in pencil before painting. Do not apply the paint too thickly on the hide or it may change the sound of the drum. Once your painting is complete, allow the drum to dry in a warm place that is *not* close to an actual heat source.

Once the paint is dry, lightly apply an acrylic spray varnish to the surface of the painting. This will protect it from the beater and offer a nice overall finish. I use a clear gloss varnish

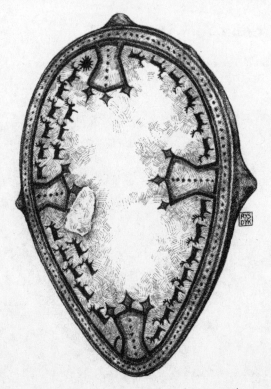

Figure 32. An Evenk drum with images of reindeer painted around its surface. This animal is herded by and considered sacred to the Evenk. (Pen and ink ©2013 Evelyn C. Rysdyk)

made by Krylon to spray my painted drum hides. Since aerosols are toxic, follow the directions on the can and spray the varnish in a well-ventilated area—preferably outdoors. You may also want to wear a paint mask or respirator while you work. Over time and through regular use, a dull spot will appear in the varnish at the point at which you beat the face of the drum. At that time, you can lightly reapply the varnish to the dull spot to continue protecting your painting.

Even after you have painted and varnished your frame drum's surface, you can treat the back of its hide with dressing to preserve it. Follow the directions in the "Caring for Your Drum" section and just work the dressing into the back of the drumhead with your hands.

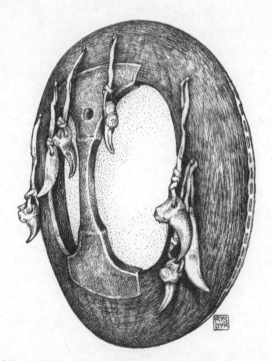

Figure 33. Back of a Sami *goavdi* that was decorated with bear claws and bear canine teeth strung on leather thongs tacked to the surface of the wooden bowl. Ethnographic Collection of the Danish National Museum in Copenhagen, Denmark. (Pen and ink ©2013 Evelyn C. Rysdyk)

Besides painting the surface, you can decorate your drum in other ways. For instance, you can tie objects to the back of the drum such as amulets, bells or jingles, or dangling tie ribbons, strips of cloth, or feathers. Your drum is part of your sacred, shamanic paraphernalia. As such, decorate it with respect to the loving spirits who assist you in your life!

Exercise: Ulchi Drum Beats

Now that you have a drum, you may want to try beating different rhythms as well as the usual journey beat. Here are some examples of the complex rhythms that I was taught when my partner and I studied with Grandfather Misha and Nadyezda Duvan, Wisdom Keeper of the Ulchi. The Ulchi drum's flexible back allows the drummer to make several different sounds (see Figure 26). Ulchi drummers use all parts of the drum—the face of the drum, the inside of the drumhead, and the rim of the drum. Here's how they do it:

F = The shaman beats on the face of the drum. Sometimes, this beat is made as a sliding beat over the drum's face with the flat surface of the fur-covered beater.

B = With the hand that is holding on to the straps inside the drum, the shaman makes a rapid movement back and forth, tapping the inside of the drumhead with the knuckles.

R = This beat is performed on the wooden rim of the drum.

f, b, r = Strike the drum with a *soft beat*.

F, B, R = Strike the drum with a *normally loud beat*.

F, B, R = Strike the drum with an *extra loud beat*.

Try making these sounds with your own drum. Then experiment with the Ulchi rhythms described below.

Ulchi Drumming Pattern	Usage	Notes
_F F F_	To open or start the drumming or journey	Three loud beats on the face of the drum.
FRRR FRRR FRRR	To build power	Grandfather Misha would repeat this beat as long as he needed to feel empowered to do the work.
FBBBB FBBBB FBBBB	To build power	This was Grandmother Tikka's method. The drum is alternately held in front of the shaman on the right side of the body (FBBBB), left side (FBBBB), then in the center in front of the body (FBBBB).
F BB F BB FFF	To honor Bear, the most powerful animal	This beat is also used very softly when asking the spirits to enter the drum prior to a journey.
BBF BBF BBFFF	To honor Tiger, the most sacred animal	This beat is also used very softly when searching for spirits on a journey.
FB RRR BBBBBBF	To drive out illness	This beat is done very vigorously with a strong intention to scare away unbeneficial energy.
FFFFFFFF F	To drive out illness	Nine regular beats on the drum, then one loud beat.
Ffff Ffff Ffff	To honor water spirits, fish spirits, or fishlike spirits	Strike the drum with a sliding, swooshy beat with a fur-covered beater. Ulchi shamans make their drum appear to "swim" back and forth as they drum when honoring these spirits.
Ffff Ffff Ffff	To honor flying spirits	This is just like the fish beat, but the drum is held over the head. The Ulchi shaman moves the drum back and forth in this position to make the drum appear to "fly."

Exercise: Your Drum Beats

If this kind of drumming appeals to you, make the following journey.

- Journey to each of your helping spirits and ask them: "How would you like me to beat my drum for you?"

Once you have made or purchased and empowered a drum, it will support you to develop your shamanic journeying and become a stronger spirit walker. The shamans of central Siberia spoke about their drums as magical horses that they "rode" into the spirit realms. Like those shamans' drums, yours is empowered and alive so it can participate in your spiritual life like a faithful partner or treasured friend.

Journey Explorations: Developing a Relationship with Your Drum

While I have already shared ways that you can care for the drum's physical body, it is also just as important to care for its unique spirit. Meeting that spirit is the very best way for you to begin a relationship with your new drum. After meeting your drum's spirit in response to your first question, you can ask the second question as well.

- Journey to a teacher or power animal to ask: "Please introduce me to the spirit that inhabits my drum." Record the content of your journey and your perceptions about what you receive.

- Journey to a teacher or power animal to ask to be taken to the drum's spirit to ask: "What is the best way to care for your spirit?" Make notes on what you receive.

To have a clearer sense of how and when it is appropriate for you to work with your drum, do the following journey:

- Journey to a teacher or power animal to ask: "What are the ways I am to use this drum in my shamanic practice?" Record the content of your journey and your perceptions about what you receive.

You will want to either make or buy a case to store and carry your new drum in. This can be constructed from leather, nylon, or cloth and may be padded to protect the drum's playing surface. Depending upon the drum's size and shape, you may be able to purchase a case, or you may have to have one specially constructed for you. Asking for your spirits' suggestions can help bring clarity about the best solution.

- Journey to a teacher or power animal to ask: "What is the best way to store my drum safely?" Make notes on what you receive.

After each journey, remember to make an offering to the spirits.

Process Questions

- Write down in your journal what it was like to create and empower your drum.

- Articulate, as best as you can, in your journal, the bodily, emotional, and spiritual sensations you receive while working with your drum.

CHAPTER 6

Flutes and Whistles

Whistling is a powerful way to interact with the spirits, and so shamans use whistling in many ways. For example, a shaman might whistle to call the spirits, accompany a journey, make a sound offering to honor a helping spirit or to "tame" a fierce spirit, drive out intrusive energies, coax an errant soul back to a patient, or signal changes in a ritual.

Perhaps it is the historic use of whistling by entranced shamans that helps to explain the many superstitious prohibitions about whistling around the globe. Among cultures from eastern Europe to Asia, it is believed that whistling by "ordinary people" could cause negative circumstances to occur. A person whistling might inadvertently call forth unbeneficial energies and spirits or bring calamities such as illness, bad luck, or a loss of wealth to themselves and the village. Similar beliefs were also prevalent in northern North America. An Alaskan Alutiiq elder once said, "We had to be very careful . . . don't whistle and things like that. . . . [T]he spirits speak in whistling. Whistling was used by shamans to call the spirits. . . . Parents caution children not to whistle, especially at night."[26] It was also believed among Arctic peoples that whistling under the aurora could call harmful spirits down from the sky.

Figure 34. Carved and painted wooden whistles are commonly used to accompany spiritual dances throughout the Northwest Coast of North America. (Pen and ink ©2013 Evelyn C. Rysdyk)

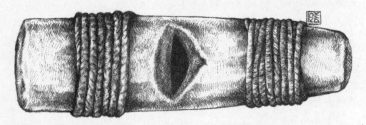

Figure 35. Alutiiq shaman's whistle made from two pieces of wood that have been carved, glued, and then lashed together. (Pen and ink ©2013 Evelyn C. Rysdyk)

All of these prohibitions are particularly interesting as whistling was seen to create the same "ailments" that would have been addressed historically by a shaman! In other words, some cultures have retained tattered memories about the power of whistling and its connection to spiritual mysteries long after shamanism was lost to them.

At the same time, cultures such as those in the Pacific Northwest of North America have used the spiritual connections of whistles to their advantage for enhancing the power of tribal dances. These dances often include transformation of the dancers into animals and birds considered to be relatives and in some cases the primordial progenitors or ancestors of the tribal clans.

The sounds of human whistling as well as those of crafted whistles and flutes are ideal for imitating bird, animal, and nature sounds. While my mother and other women in my family sang sweetly or hummed as they worked, several of the menfolk were masterful whistlers. With no other instrument than their own lips and breath, they could imitate songbirds and raptors as well as produce marvelous melodies. My paternal grandfather had an enormous repertoire of incredible chirping and trilling birdsongs he would intersperse with recognizable tunes from his youth. My father's whistling called us in from our play, accompanied his work tasks, entertained him as he drove, and his spot-on, red-tailed hawk impersonation never failed to chase pigeons into flight! The wealth of sounds I heard as a child were such a source of fascination to me that I imitated them until I became a whistler, too. My way of calling spirits is through whistling, and I also relish whistling as I work on creative tasks.

Whether our long-ago ancestors first learned to whistle because they were entranced by the sounds of nature or simply noticed that they could make sounds by breathing through pursed lips, it is clear that they eventually crafted flutes and whistles to make music. While the human voice may arguably be the earliest musical "instrument"—with rhythm instruments like simple drums a close second—flutes and whistles have been around since our ancient human ancestors first began to colonize Europe. The most recently discovered examples of flutes date from the Aurignacian culture of the Upper Paleolithic that existed in Europe and southwestern Asia 45,000 to 35,000 years ago and are approximately 35,000 years old.

Figure 36. The Hohle Fels flute was carved over 35,000 years ago from a griffon vulture bone by Upper Paleolithic people. (Pen and ink ©2013 Evelyn C. Rysdyk)

These flutes carved from griffon vulture bones, swan bones, or mammoth ivory are sophisticated instruments capable of the same tones and harmonic variety of contemporary flutes. Finds unearthed in southwestern Germany such as in the Hohle Fels cave are undisputable proof that our ancestors' world was filled with music. The Hohle Fels flute is about eight and a half inches long and so would have produced a high, tin whistle-like sound. One can certainly imagine listening to the haunting sounds of flute music echoing around a cave while animals painted on the walls "danced" in the flickering firelight!

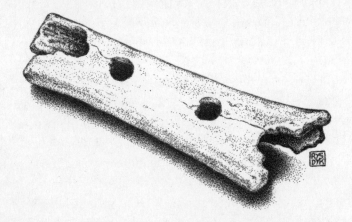

Figure 37. The late Pleistocene Divje Babe flute is made from an *Ursus spelaeus*, or cave bear, femur and is over 43,000 years old. Collection of the National Museum of Slovenia. (Pen and ink ©2013 Evelyn C. Rysdyk)

An older, still disputed object made from a juvenile cave bear femur dates from the Neanderthal period in Europe approximately 45,000 years ago. Known as the Divje Babe flute, this artifact discovered in Slovenia may push our flute-making skills to an even earlier time. Professional musician Ljuben Dimkaroski, a member of the Ljubljana Opera Orchestra, has successfully played a reproduction of the Divje Babe flute created under the auspices of the National Museum of Slovenia.[27]

Later period bone flutes have been found around the globe. Early Irish examples were made from swan bones, while examples from other regions have used various bird, deer, sheep, and other bones.

Among the Native American peoples of the Great Plains, eagle-bone whistles are an integral part of the Sundance ceremony. These shrill whistles are used to give the dancers the eagle's courage, to carry their prayers "on eagle's wings" to the creator, and to assist the dancers' connections to the spiritual realms as they danced on Unce Maka, Grandmother Earth. The late Lakota elder Grandfather Wallace Black Elk even asserted that whistles given to his people by the Star Nations were capable of generating sounds that would make megaliths light enough to lift by hand.

I have many whistles and flutes that I use in my own shamanic practice. While I have made some of them, I have also purchased beautiful examples as well. For instance, I have several fine Native American cedar flutes that have a beautiful and sweet voices, and I also have a bone flute I made myself. While the cedar flutes are capable of playing perfect, harmonious melodies, I reach for the bone flute just as often, as its unusual voice is perfect for playing to certain nature spirits who have told me in journeys that they prefer those sounds.

Exercise: Making a Bone Flute

Across the many millennia of our collective human history, hollow reeds, bones, bamboo, pieces of wood, clay, stone, and other materials have been successfully crafted into flutes.

Having a flute to play out in nature is a special experience. I have noticed that the spirits of nature respond well to the sound of a flute, and birds often come closer to me while I am playing. Making this kind of flute is a challenging project, but I found that it was worth the time and energy. While making my bone flute, I felt a profound connection to my Paleolithic ancestors.

No two handmade flutes are the same. Each produces its own unique sound based on a number of factors, including hole placement, bore diameter, and tube length. Since no two bones have the same length or bore diameter, locating the finger hole placements is very difficult. I found this to be a hit-or-miss procedure, as it must have been in the earliest days. My bone flute makes clear tones but not on any traditional scale. However, the result is haunting, atonal music that I feel is perfect for my spirit work.

If you are willing to experiment a bit with different bones and hole placements, creating a bone flute can be a rewarding project. As before, prepare yourself by reading all of the instructions before tackling this challenging craft adventure. You may find it very helpful to look at the videos that flute craftsman Vlad Cardema has posted on YouTube. While he is making wooden flutes, many of the procedures and challenges are exactly the same when carving a bone flute.

Materials and Tools

- Fresh sheep, goat, elk, or deer leg bones from the butcher

- A hacksaw

- A large, nonreactive, porcelain-clad or glass stovetop cooking pot

- Powdered clothes-washing detergent

- A large glass or glazed pottery mixing bowl

- Enough hydrogen peroxide from the drugstore to completely fill the bowl

- Several sheets of sandpaper (60, 100, and 150 grit)

- Ten-inch round file, six-inch round file, six-inch half-round and six-inch flat file

- A variable-speed drill

- Eighth-inch and quarter-inch drill bits

- Beeswax and olive oil

- Small, heatproof bowl

- Skewer or stick small enough to insert in the bore of your flute

Making Your Flute Base

1. Clean the bones in advance of making your flute. It is best to clean a few bones at the same time so that you can experiment with flute designs. To clean a bone, scrape off any remaining meat, carefully cut off both "knuckle" ends with a hacksaw, and remove the marrow. Next, simmer them for two hours in a large pot of water to which two tablespoons of powdered detergent have been added. This will degrease the bones. When the time is up, drain the water, rinse the bones, and let them cool. Take the bones and place them into a nonreactive, glass or porcelain bowl. Cover them in hydrogen peroxide and allow them to soak overnight. Afterwards, rinse them thoroughly and allow them to dry.

2. When you are ready to make your flute, begin by sanding both cut ends to smooth out any rough edges. This will make all the subsequent steps easier to perform.

3. Use the round file to smooth out the inside of the bone.

4. The next step is to decide which end will be the mouthpiece. Choose the end of the bone that is more elliptical.

5. Make the aperture or notch that will divert your breath to create sound. Using your round file, make a notch a quarter

inch into the mouthpiece end. File it so that it rises onto the face of the flute on an angle. (See Vlad Cardema's videos on YouTube for a visual on this step.) Keep testing your notch until you can make a pleasing tone by blowing over the notch.

6. Smooth the edges of the notch where it meets the end of the bone so that it will be more comfortable when played.

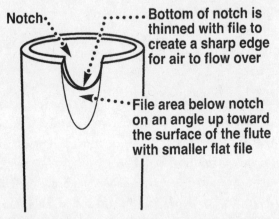

Notch

Bottom of notch is thinned with file to create a sharp edge for air to flow over

File area below notch on an angle up toward the surface of the flute with smaller flat file

Figure 38. The flute notch is filed into the end of the bone you have designated as the mouthpiece. It is about a quarter inch deep.

7. Now using that flat file, flatten the back of the mouthpiece that will lie against your lip.

8. Using sandpaper, smooth the entire mouthpiece.

Making the Finger Holes

It is easier to create a flute by drilling only one finger hole. This kind of flute will make three notes plus the additional tones that occur when the finger hole is only partially covered. This is referred to as a "half-hole" note and is a common way to get more notes from a diatonic instrument, such as a Native American flute or Japanese *shakuhachi*. One note is the open flute, covering the finger hole halfway plays the second note, the third is played by completely covering the finger hole, and another tone is made by also partially covering the bottom end of the flute.

If you decide that you'd rather try your hand at drilling multiple finger holes in your flute, there are some guidelines that can help you. The diagram here explains the most favorable positions of the finger holes. To make holes following this diagram, you must first measure the length of the flute from the bottom of the notch to the bottom end of the flute body. The finger holes are then positioned based upon the percentages of that flute length measurement. In other words, the second finger hole is positioned at exactly half (50 percent) of the length from bottom of notch to bottom end of the flute.

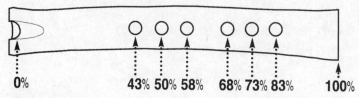

Figure 39. This diagram shows calculations for positioning the finger holes for your flute.

Tuning the Flute

It is important to note that in spite of all your best efforts to carefully measure hole placements, the sounds made by these holes will most likely be a bit off-key. As a result, you may need to alter the finger holes a bit to get a pleasing tone.

There are several important rules for tuning:

A hole will give a higher note if it is placed closer to the notch. It will give a lower note if placed farther away.

A hole will also give a higher note if made larger. It will give a lower note if smaller.

You can "raise" or "sharpen" a note by filing the edge of the hole closer to the notch. You can "lower" or "flatten" the note by filing the edge of the hole farther from the notch.

Finishing the Flute

Once you are satisfied with your flute, you may want to give it a coat of a mix of beeswax and olive oil. To do this, place a bit of beeswax in a small, heatproof bowl and melt it with care in the microwave. Stir in a small amount of olive oil to make the wax more fluid. While this mixture is still a bit warm, rub it into the bone with a cotton cloth. Wrap a bit of the cloth on a stick or skewer to wax the inside of the bone, as well. Once the wax cools, buff your flute with a clean, soft cloth until the bone shines.

Exercise: Journey to Empower Your New Flute

At this point, your completed flute will need to be enlivened and empowered for its sacred purpose. If you have purchased your flute, you can follow these same instructions to dedicate your new instrument for sacred work.

When you are ready to dedicate your flute, make a gratitude offering to the spirits. Pay special attention to your ancestors as well as the animal whose bone you used. Call with your heart to bring your power animal and teacher to you. When you feel ready, merge with your teacher and begin to sing your power song while holding the flute in your hands. Once you feel the full power of your teacher, begin playing the flute with the intention of blowing your teacher's spirit into the flute's body. When the process feels complete, unmerge from your teacher and return to ordinary reality.

Upon your return at the callback signal, take ample time to sit with the experience prior to recording it in your notebook. Remember to go outside and make an offering of thanks to the ancestors, the original owner of the bone, and your helping spirits.

Caring for your flute. Do a journey to your teacher and ask for suggestions for how you can care for the spirit of your flute. For instance, your whistle may require "feeding" or need to be placed out in the wind at regular intervals to reconnect with the elementals of the winds and air.

Figure 40. Peruvian shaman, or *paqo*, Fredy "Puma" Quispe Singona playing a traditional *quena* in the Andes Mountains. A bone flute is played in the same manner. (Pen and ink ©2013 Evelyn C. Rysdyk)

Once you have empowered your flute and learned from your helping spirits about what care it requires, it is time to get better acquainted. The very best way to get to know the spirit of your flute is to play it outside! Music can bewitch human beings and connect us to the beauty of All That Is. The same sweet music connects us with spirits that enliven the natural world. Stories recalled about the faeries or Middle World spirits in Europe speak about the power of music. Folktales suggest faerie music has many marvelous powers such as the ability to coax the plants to grow, enrapture animals, make things or beings manifest or disappear, and cause creatures to either wake or fall in a deep slumber.

Human-made music is also powerful and a wonderful offering to the spirits. Singing and the playing of instruments are ways we can reciprocate for all the beauty we are given. When we make music in these most ancient of ways, we gain a closer relationship with the Middle World nature spirits, and the spirits of the animals, birds, plants, and trees.

When I sing or play instruments in nature, everything around me seems much more lively. I feel as though the birds sing along with my flute, the rustling trees create harmony, and the animals approach much closer to me.

Exercise: Playing from the Heart

Choose a time and place when you will not be interrupted while outside. Bring your offering materials and your flute to a beautiful spot and settle into a comfortable position. Make an offering and then spend a few minutes breathing and connecting to the place. Once you feel fully present with the place you have chosen, pick up your flute. Hold it to your heart for a few moments. Once you feel connected, raise it to begin playing. Don't worry about what notes you play. Just allow your heart to work your fingers and your breath to make the sounds. Keep a lighthearted feeling and continue playing for an hour. When the hour is through, gently return to silence and listen with your heart. Notice everything around you and allow your self to fill with gratitude for the gifts you have been given before, during, and after you played. When you feel complete, do the following journeys.

Journey Explorations

- Journey with a teacher or power animal to the spirits of your place in nature to ask these questions:

  - "What was your experience of my music?"

  - "How may I nurture my connections with you through playing my flute?"

- Take separate journeys to a tree, an animal, and a bird on the land near to your home to ask them what sounds they would like as an offering.

Record the content of your journeys and your reflections about the experience of playing outside.

Other Kinds of Music

Since the 1970s we have seen a resurgence of interest in folk music and the ancient instruments on which these songs were originally played. Today we see many indigenous musical styles being honored, preserved, played, and fused with music from other geographic regions. As a result of this renewed interest, formerly unknown instruments of historic or unique regional interest are much more widely available.

For instance, in South America, many kinds of traditional flutes and whistles are popular. Pan flutes, or *zampoñas*, ocarinas, clay whistles, and end-blown *quena* flutes are all commonly played in modern-day Peru. However there are some very special instruments that have purposes that transcend simple music.

The *huaco silbador*, or whistling vessel, is a shamanic instrument that dates back to Pre-Columbian times. In the *curanderisimo* tradition of the Peruvian north coast, whistling vessels or *huaco silbadors* are used by the *curanderas* to call in the spirits for protection and/or healing. The *curanderas* and *curanderos* of this tradition are shamanic healers who usually construct an elaborate altar, called a *mesa*, for their healing ceremonies. These *mesas* have dozens of power objects placed on them to assist the healer in her or his work. Along with swords, wands, bottles of perfume, herbs, and other objects, a *huaco silbador* is often present. Depending upon their shape or dedicated purpose, these vessels may be used to summon different spirit helpers and also to provide a "home" for the spirit in this realm. For instance, an animal-shaped vessel may contain the spirit of the animal, be used to summon the animal spirit to assist the *curandera*, or be dedicated for a different purpose such as clearing the space in which the healing is to occur. As with other shamanic objects, it is the enlivening process carried out by the shaman that gives the vessels power.

Figure 41. A contemporary reproduction of a 1,000-year-old Peruvian whistling vessel, or *huaco silbador*. (Pen and ink ©2013 Evelyn C. Rysdyk)

The sounds of several *huaco silbadors* used together may assist a spirit walker in moving into other realms. While individually the vessels seem quite shrill, when played in a group they produce complex harmonics and vibrations with psychoacoustic properties. The extraordinary sounds produced by the vessels encourage an expanded state of consciousness offering a slightly different approach to the shamanic journey than a rattle or drum. The overtones and harmonics have been described as resembling whale songs, chattering monkeys, insects buzzing, or murmuring voices or winds. Strangely, the otherworldly sounds emanating from the vessels seem to occur both inside as well as outside of the body. This is most profound when a person is playing a vessel but may also be experienced by other participants in a ceremony. These internally experienced sounds are what are most remarked upon by participants and contribute to consciousness-altering experiences. We have had participants say that they continue to "hear" the vibrations in their bodies for several days after the initial experience, and some individuals have found that these sounds also have profound healing properties.

A Whistle of Your Own

As we have been discussing, whistling can take many forms and be used for many purposes by the spirit walker. Those of you who use the Spirit Passages *Shamanic Journey Drumming* recording to accompany your journeys have heard my whistling. As a lifelong whistler, I am comfortable using my mouth and breath to make a wide variety of musical sounds. When I honor the spirits prior to doing shamanic work, I shake my rattle and whistle. I use my whistling as an auditory offering to the spirits of nature and even when I perform healings.

Sometimes, I also use a physical whistle to make sounds. Along with my many flutes, I have wooden, metal, and bone whistles that I use in my practice. These can be easily carried in a pocket to play outdoors or to call a helping spirit and during a ceremony or healing. I even have one I play very softly to encourage the birds to sing!

The directions that follow will help you to make a simple wooden whistle that can complement your spirit walker practice.

Exercise: Making a Wooden Spirit Whistle

A whistle dedicated to shamanic work is a useful part of the spirit walker's tool kit. Making your own is a rewarding experience and allows you to create exactly what you desire. These instructions are for creating a whistle from a length of dry tree branch. In choosing the proper branch, look for something of the right diameter that has been blown down by the wind but is still very sturdy. It is best if the length is straight with no other branches extending from it. Before you begin making your whistle, decide if you want to remove the bark or leave it in place. Smooth bark trees such as maple or birch can work well with the bark left intact. Read through all of the directions carefully before you begin. Once you are ready to start working on your whistle, welcome the helping spirits into your workspace and make an offering to them in gratitude for their support.

Materials and Tools

- A length of dry tree branch approximately three-quarters or an inch thick and at least four inches long.

- A sharp knife for whittling

- Sandpaper

- A drill and long five-sixteenths-inch bit (You will be drilling a three and a half-inch-long hole.)

- Masking tape

- Pencil

- A piece of five-sixteenths of an inch dowel at least two inches long (You'll only be using about three-quarters of an inch of the dowel but the prescribed length makes it easier to handle.)

- A fine-blade wood saw

- Wood glue

- Vise (This is very useful to to hold the stick while it is being drilled, but if one is not available, you may fix the stick vertically with wood clamps and have someone hold the clamps for you, making sure that all hands are well away from the stick and the drill!)

Making Your Whistle

1. Trim the stick you've chosen so that it is four inches long.

2. Smooth the cut ends of the stick with sandpaper and refer to the diagram to perform the next steps.

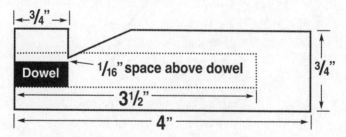

Figure 42. Cutaway diagram of the wooden whistle.

3. Holding the stick vertically, drill a five-sixteenths-inch hole down the center of the stick. Go slowly and make this hole three and a half inches deep. To make sure that you get this measurement right, place a piece of masking tape on the

drill bit at the three and a half inch mark. This will give you a guide to know when your hole is the right depth.

4. Once you are finished drilling, decide what will be the top face of your whistle. Make a pencil mark on this side.

5. Holding the stick so that you can look in the hole you have drilled, carefully measure the distance from the top surface of your whistle face to the top of the drilled hole.

6. Measure in three-quarters of an inch from the drilled end and make a cut that goes down into the stick one-sixteenth of an inch deeper than your measurement above. In other words, your cut will be intersecting the drilled chamber a tiny bit. To make sure your cut will be the proper depth, place a piece of masking tape on your saw blade at the correct depth.

7. Whittle back the sound hole "wedge" as shown in the diagram.

8. Now it is time to fit the dowel. Begin by sanding *one* side of the dowel flat. Sanding should only remove one-quarter to one-third of the diameter of the dowel.

Figure 43. This diagram shows the dowel inside of the hole of the whistle.

9. Slide the dowel rod into the hole in the stick with the flat side facing the side of the stick where you cut the sound hole. The end of the dowel should be near the spot where the wedge-shaped cut intersects the hole. See the diagram. The dowel will stick out the end of the whistle body for now; it will be trimmed to size later. Try blowing into the whistle. You may have to move the dowel in and out slightly to get the whistle to make a good sound.

10. Get the dowel positioned so it makes the best sound, then cut off the exposed part of the dowel while it is still in the stick. Remove the dowel, put a thin coat of wood glue on the rounded part and return it to the hole. Use your knife blade to push the dowel into place. Make sure the whistle makes the right sound; if not, reposition the dowel as needed before the glues sets and dries.

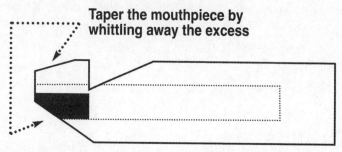

Figure 44. Whittle the mouthpiece end until it is comfortable.

11. Once the glue is dry, shape the whistle's mouthpiece by cutting away some of the back face of the whistle's body and sanding the edges so that they are tapered and smooth.

12. You may wish to secure a lanyard or cord to your whistle so you can hang it around your neck.

Exercise: Journey to Empower Your New Whistle

At this point, your completed whistle needs to be enlivened and empowered for its sacred purpose.

When you are ready to dedicate your new whistle to your spirit walker practice, make a gratitude offering to the spirits. Honor that which you have been given and your connections to the world of spiritual power. Call with your heart to bring your power animal and teacher to you. When you feel ready, merge with your teacher and begin to sing your power song while holding the whistle. Once you feel the full power of your teacher, begin blowing the whistle with the intention of blowing the teacher's spirit into the whistle's body. When the process feels complete, unmerge from your teacher and return yourself to ordinary reality.

Upon your return at the callback signal, take ample time to sit with the experience prior to recording it in your notebook. Remember to go outside and make an offering of thanks. Let your heart fill with gratitude for the gifts you have received in this experience and place your offering on the Earth with reverence.

Caring for your whistle. Do a journey to your teacher and ask for suggestions for how you can care for the spirit of your whistle. For instance, your whistle may require "feeding" or need to be placed out in the wind at regular intervals to reconnect with the spirits of the air.

Journey Explorations

- Journey to a teacher or power animal to ask: "What are the ways I am to use this whistle in my shamanic practice?"

Record the content of your journey and your perceptions
about what you receive.

- Journey to a teacher or power animal to ask: "What is the
best way to care for my new instrument's spirit?"

After each journey, make an audible offering to the spirits of
nature with your whistle.

Process Questions

- Write down in your journal what it was like to create and
empower your flute and/or whistle.

- Articulate, as best as you can, in your journal, the bodily,
emotional, and spiritual sensations you receive while playing these instruments.

CHAPTER 7

Prayer Beads and *Malas*

Strings of beads are used by the faithful of many spiritual traditions. These tools are common to Buddhists, Hindus, Sikhs, Muslims, and Catholics as well as many shamanic practitioners. Typically, these rosaries, or *malas*, are used to focus or count a prescribed numbers of prayers, mantras, or meditations. Each time the prayer or mantra is spoken aloud, one bead is run through the fingers. This physical action assists a spirit walker in more fully embodying prayers.

Malas, or prayer beads, may be made of many materials. Wood, shell, root, crystal, seeds, bone, horn, pottery, precious stones, amber, and metal are all used to make prayer bead strands. For some practitioners, the spiritual purpose of the *mala* can determine what substance is chosen. For instance, if you are working with peaceful deities, you might choose a *mala* with white or crystal beads, while if you were chanting mantras to increase life span or deepen wisdom a gold, copper, silver, or amber *mala* might be picked.

Typically *malas* used by Himalayan practitioners have 108 beads. The number 108 is thought to have special numerological significance and considered special and sacred in Hinduism, Buddhism, Taoism, and other religions such as Islam, which refers to God with this number. Since 108 is divisible by three, manifestations such as past-present-future, birth-life-death, and body-mind-spirit and the three shamanic realms of the Upper, Middle, and Lower Worlds are contained within it.

Malas such as those worn on the wrist or ones with over-size beads may have fewer than 108 beads. These *malas* typically contain either fifty-four or twenty-seven beads, since, respectively, these numbers are either a half or quarter of the requisite count allowing the practitioner to easily total up the necessary repetitions.

Prayer beads may also have counter beads strung along the length of the strand to keep track of the specific number of circuits made around the *mala*. Known as *chupshed* or *chopshee* in Nepal, these special counting beads can be assigned the role of tracking of hundreds or thousands of prayers.

Shamanic Uses of Prayer Beads

A spirit walker can use a prayer bead string for several purposes. A *mala* may assist the spirit walker in shifting states of consciousness or grounding and centering after working with the spirits, be worn as a part of a shaman's personal ritual garb, or be used in personal prayer rituals or to honor specific spirits. As with other shamanic paraphernalia, once the prayer beads are empowered, they may also perform healing or ritual work on behalf the shaman.

As Michael Winkelman, PhD, states in his book *Shamanism: The Neural Ecology of Consciousness and Healing*:

> *The shaman is a technician of consciousness who utilizes those potentials for healing and for personal and social transformations.*

The art of disciplined alteration of consciousness is essential for a spirit walker to accomplish her or his work. While you may be most familiar with the use of repetitive drumming or rattling to expand awareness, the repetition of words or chants can have a similar effect. Indeed, it is common for shamans to sing while drumming to enhance the depth of the shamanic trance. However, it is possible to enter the shamanic state of consciousness through singing or chanting alone. After chanting for a few minutes, the consciousness of a disciplined shamanic practitioner can easily slip into the realm of the spirits. I can attest firsthand to the mesmerizing and consciousness-altering effect of chanting. I was fortunate to visit the last Tibetan shaman, or *lhapa*, Nyima Dhondup at his home in Nepal. All during the healing ceremony, which was attended by several other people, an elder was chanting his mantras in an adjacent home. Since the weather was warm, the sounds of his voice traveled into the *lhapa*'s house through the open windows. Even though I wasn't the one making the sounds, the elder's chanting lifted me into the shamanic state of consciousness. This allowed me to easily observe the spiritual aspect of the *lhapa*'s healing work and see the spirits who assisted him.

This use of chanting to alter states of consciousness is also a "two-way street;" counting on a *mala* can also have the effect of bringing the bearer into laser-like focus on the present moment. By fingering the beads and counting or chanting, the practitioner slows the breath, and the perceptions of the moment can become expanded and clear. This brings the spirit walker more keenly into ordinary reality.

My Nepalese *jhankri* friend Bhola Banstola keeps a strand of prayer beads close at hand when he is teaching workshops. He reaches for them after he has drummed, danced, and sung forth his power. While his intent is to express his gratitude, he is also settling back into his body and his ordinary reality consciousness through working the beads. Used in this way, his *mala* helps him to attain a calmer, centered, and more grounded affect, which is more suitable for presenting information.

Prayer Beads as Ritual Attire

Among Himalayan shamans, *malas* of *rudraksha* seeds are not only used for meditation and prayer but also as part of a shaman's protective, ceremonial attire. Bhola wears several very large *malas* crossed over his heart along with a strand of large brass bells. The *malas* are made of a combination of *rudraksha* seeds and the seeds from the *Sapindus mukorossi*, or soap nut tree, indigenous to the Himalayan mountain ranges. Soap nuts have been used since time immemorial for washing clothes and as a gentle natural wash for body care. In spiritual terms, a rosary made from these seeds helps to cleanse the area around the shaman, keeping it clear of all negative influences.

Rudraksha seeds are considered sacred to the Hindu god Shiva. The word *rudraksha* is a combination of the Sanskrit words for *Shiva* (*Rudra*) and *eyes* (*aksh*) and means the "tears of Shiva." The deity shed these tears in a moment of bliss. The practice of Nepalese shamanism is both animistic and polytheistic. It honors the spirits of nature, the ancestors, and tutelary spirits as well as many gods and goddesses who control the forces of nature and the workings of the cosmos. The god Shiva is one such deity acknowledged by Himalayan shamans as the supreme deity or creator.

Figure 45. *Rudraksha* seed. (Pen and ink ©2013 Evelyn C. Rysdyk)

Rudraksha malas are also traditionally used to subdue or "tame" harmful energies. Since shamans are responsible for combating chaos, healing illness, and moving the spirits of the dead from our world, they are often thought of as gaining mastery over unbeneficial spirits. This idea is common in many areas of the world. Among central Asian shamans, for example, a ceremonial horse switch is part of their traditional paraphernalia to control harmful energies. As a rider might control a horse, in the same way, *rudraksha malas* are used by Himalayan *jhankris* to subdue disease-causing or disruptive spirits.

By using *rudraksha*, which are sacred to Shiva, and soap nut seeds together, Bhola is ritually enfolding himself in the blessing and protection of the divine while maintaining a spiritually clean space around himself as he does his shamanic work.

Honoring Specific Spirits

Some practitioners wear prayer beads to merge with their helping spirits or for the purpose of honoring specific spirit helpers. In these cases, the materials used for the prayer beads may also have a deep significance to the spirit walker.

For instance, a person working with northern European shamanic practices such as *seiðr,* may choose amber since it is considered sacred to Freyja, the goddess of prophecy. Others may choose quartz crystal to contact light beings or to honor a spirit of a place or for use during transfiguration.[28] Those working with the Norse runes or the Celtic *ogham* alphabet might have beads that are inscribed with these symbols.

I have seen a beautiful example of a *mala* made from jet with a carved raven head as a central bead. This set of beads connects the bearer to a primary power animal and is held while the spirit walker is journeying. The example in Figure 46 is of a wrist *mala* containing beads that represent the elements of nature and a claw from the shaman's primary protector.

Figure 46. A contemporary shaman's wrist *mala* composed of beads of fossilized coral, a "deer's eye" seed (*Mucuna sloanei*), amber, fossilize mammoth ivory, and bone beads, as well as an Inuit fishing weight made from fossilized walrus ivory and a polar bear claw. (The claw is from a piece of taxidermy that dates from before the 1972 Marine Mammal Protection Act ban. Pen and ink ©2013 Evelyn C. Rysdyk)

The *Mala* as Divination Tool

In Tibetan Buddhism and Mongolian shamanism, *malas* are also used as divination tools.[29] In these rituals, a *mala* is picked up with both hands in a random place on the strand. Spirit walkers count off beads in groups of three as they move both hands together. They continue counting until one, two, or three beads are left between the hands. This number is marked down, and then the process is done a second time.

In this tradition, one bead remaining is referred to as a *Falcon*. This is a positive sign indicating good luck and success.

Two beads remaining between the hands is a *Raven*. This is considered a sign indicating an unbeneficial outcome or bad luck in a situation.

The three-bead grouping is a *Snow Lion*. This suggests that the person making the inquiry is supported by the spirits and that results will be steady and positive.

The diviner then takes into consideration the numbers from the two rounds of counting and uses the following formula to determine the will of the spirits:

- Falcon after Falcon (1 after 1)

  - Everything about the situation is favorable.

- Falcon after Raven (1 after 2)

  - Every wish will be fulfilled, and danger will be avoided.

- Falcon after Snow Lion (1 after 3)

  - Spirit's help is at hand; make an offering to the spirits.

- Raven after Falcon (2 after 1)

  - This is a bad omen, and so more offerings and protections must be done to shift the situation.

- Raven after Raven (2 after 2)

  - Dark times are on the horizon, and money loss may ensue.

- Raven after Snow Lion (2 after 3)

  - Obstacles are present, and legal problems may ensue.

- Snow Lion after Falcon (3 after 1)

  - This indicates positive outcomes in all situations, increased fertility and wealth.

- Snow Lion after Raven (3 after 2)

  - This indicates that unexpected boons, and monetary gains will ensue. Danger will be escaped.

- Snow Lion after Snow Lion (3 after 3)

  - Prosperity in all forms is imminent.

Exercise: Making a Strand of Prayer Beads

While you may want to purchase a *mala* and then dedicate it to your shamanic practice, it is also very rewarding to make a highly personal strand of prayer beads. These beads can more closely represent the spirits you work with or be designed with your specific purpose in mind.

Before you begin the project, spend time thinking about how you want to use your *mala*. Will you be using it for protection? Is it going to be a part of your shamanic attire? Do you wish to have this *mala* for chanting a specific mantra or prayer? Consider your intentions well, and then do journeys to ask your spirits about what *they* would like you to include in the strand as well as what number of beads will be used.

Materials and Tools

- The number and variety of beads you would like to include in your *mala*

- Appropriate beading cord (If you are making a wrist *mala*, you may want to use an elasticized bead cord that will stretch over your hand and return to a size suitable for your wrist.)

- A needle that will pass through the opening in your beads while it is threaded

- A special bead or pendant to use as a "guru bead"

Making Your *Mala*

As you have done with other projects, create a time and space for your work. Prepare yourself and that space so that the project can be completed in a prayerful manner.

1. Thread a length of cord that is longer than your finished *mala* will be on the needle and knot the end so that the threaded beads will not slide off.

2. Start by threading your guru bead or pendant.

3. Thread each subsequent bead while thanking the spirit it represents or honoring the purpose you have for the *mala*.

4. When you have strung all of your beads, knot the ends of the cord together securely.

5. Empower the *mala* for its purpose, and then do the following journeywork.

Journey Explorations

- Journey to a teacher or power animal to ask: "What are the ways I am to use this strand of prayer beads in my shamanic practice?" Record the content of your journey and your perceptions about what you receive.

- Your *mala* it is now a living being that requires special care. Journey to a teacher or power animal to ask: "What is the best way to care for my *mala*'s spirit?"

After each journey, make an offering to the spirits represented in your *mala*.

Process Questions

- After using your prayer beads for a month, take some time to write your impressions of working with the *mala*.

Record your thoughts and feelings in your journal.

CHAPTER 8

Bells

Sound is one way to express and experience the intangible. Sound arises from silence into a manifestation that can be experienced in the physical world. In this way, sound is an excellent example of the process whereby the ephemeral spirit gives birth to our tangible reality—what a physicist might describe as vibrations producing the particles of physical matter. For the spirit walker, this means that sound can be used with intention for many different purposes.

A spirit walker may choose bells instead of rattles for preparing a space for shamanic work, to welcome the spirits, to clear a space of negative influences, for making a sound offering to the spirit walker's helping spirits, or even as a part of ritual attire.

Clearing or Preparing

Himalayan shamans as well as practitioners of the Bon religion use a flat, cymbal-like bell called a *shang* (Tibetans refer to it as a *gchang*) to broadcast or throw their intentions through the air. These bells are held with the opening facing upward like a shallow bowl. *Shang* bells are rung while the shaman creates sacred space, performs a healing, or banishes ghosts and other unbeneficial spirits. They range in size from around four inches to more than twenty inches and are made from a similar alloy as the bells used in Buddhist dharma practice.

In Tibetan Buddhism, which still retains some aspects of the earlier shamanic traditions of the region, a bell is held in the left hand during ritual prayer. This bell represents the Great Emptiness from which all form originates and returns. Represented by the deity Prajnaparamita, the Great Mother, this emptiness is thought of as the true reality behind all existence. In this way, the bell is a feminine symbol, an overturned chalice from which all life flows. Ringing the bell is a way to bring a practitioner into greater awareness of the true nature of reality.

Figure 47. Tibetan Buddhist bell. (Pen and ink ©2013 Evelyn C. Rysdyk)

Sound Offerings

In Buddhism, bells are also used as a form of sound offering to peaceful deities. Sweet sound is thought to appease and attract these beings. This is very much in keeping with the way sound can be used by a spirit walker. For example, bells can be used in honoring your helping spirits, played in gratitude for their assistance, and entice beneficial spirits into a location that has become dispirited. Transcendent Middle World nature spirits may be honored in this fashion.

During special shamanic rituals in northeastern Thailand and Laos, the feminine sky deity Phi Faa is honored with sound.[30] Phi Faa is considered the primordial being who created the Earth and so is invoked for her protection and honored in healing rituals. The sounds used during the Phi Faa healing ritual direct her healing energies to the patient.

Wearing Bells

The use of bells is particularly widespread among Asian shamans. Like my friend Bhola, most Nepalese and Tibetan shamans wear bells as a part of their work. These bells are tied on belts around the waist and strung on chains to wear over the shoulder and across the body, bandolier-style. While contemporary examples of these shamanic bandoliers use lighter weight bells, some older examples have many, heavy three- to four-inch-tall cast metal bells along their length. Typically, a shaman may wear more than one of these belts while working. Carried as they are on the torso, these bells ring when the shaman begins to shake. This shaking is a sign that the healing spirits have taken possession of the shaman's body.

Figure 48. "Tiger" bells are used in Nepalese shamanic belts and bandoliers. (Pen and ink ©2013 Evelyn C. Rysdyk)

Figure 49. Kham Magar shaman from Nepal wearing a bandolier of bells. (Photo: Mariarosa "Mimi" Genitrini and Bhola Banstola)

My Ulchi teacher Grandfather Misha also wore a series of long, hand-wrought iron bells as a part of his attire. (See chapter 17 for a full description of his ritual garb.) The bells are a part of a bustle, or *yompa*, worn at the back of his waist during his shamanic duties. Like Bhola's bandoliers, this bustle would accompany Grandfather's dances and songs to the spirits.

Other Siberian shamans have bells sewn to their costumes or hanging from the inside of their frame drums. These bells are made of iron and sometimes hung on iron rings in groups of three.

Exercise: Choosing a Bell

To find out if a bell is "right" for your shamanic work, do a journey to ask your teacher or power animal. If it is suggested that a bell would be useful to you, ask the spirits what purpose the bell will serve, as this may impact the kind of bell you require.

Figure 50. A Mongolian shaman's wrought-iron bells. (Pen and ink ©2013 Evelyn C. Rysdyk)

As you did with your drum, take ample opportunities to try bells so that you can find a good fit! Some shamanic practitioners use bells in place of rattles. They ring them to call the spirits, to accompany ceremonies, to support their journeys, and as a part of their healing practices. You may need a small bell to sew on your jacket, one that is easy to hold, or a large bell that is designed for mounting on a post in the yard. Perhaps it is one that needs to have a loud voice to clear unbeneficial energies or a light and musical tinkling sound to work with the Middle World nature spirits. As with so much on this path, the use of bells is highly personal and unique to each practitioner.

Exercise: Empowering Your Bell

When you have the right bell, it is time to empower it so that it is dedicated to sacred purpose. Start by making a gratitude offering to the spirits. Honor the spirits of the directions, your power animal, and spirit teacher. Enter into a journey and connect with your heart to your power animal. When you feel ready, sing your power song and merge with your power animal here in the Middle World while holding the bell. Then, take the bell to the Upper World and ask your spirit teacher there to merge with your bell. When you feel the teacher enter the bell, begin to sing and dance with the enlivened bell. When the process is complete, ring or tap the rhythm of the callback on the bell, unmerge, and return yourself to ordinary reality.

Upon your return at the callback signal, take ample time to sit with the experience prior to recording it in your notebook. Remember to go outside and make an offering of thanks. Let your heart fill with gratitude for the gifts you have received in this experience and lovingly place an offering on the Earth.

Journey Explorations

- Journey to a teacher or power animal to ask: "What are the ways I am to use this bell in my shamanic practice?" Record the content of your journey and your perceptions about what you receive.

- Journey to a teacher or power animal to ask: "What is the best way to care for my bell's spirit?" Make notes on what you receive.

After each journey, make an offering to the spirits while gently ringing your bell.

Process Questions

- After using your bell for a month, take some time to write your impressions of working with its sound.

Record your thoughts and feelings in your journal.

CHAPTER 9

Shaman Bundles, Talismans, and Prayer Bundles

I n many traditions, the spirit walker has a group of sacred objects or talismans that support her or his connection to power. These bundles may represent and contain the spirits who work with the shaman, be part of the spirit walker's or tribal group's protection, stand in for the shaman's own spirit during a ceremony, or be used as an offering to the spirits.

The Shaman Bundle

In the process of unearthing ancient burials around the globe, archaeologists have discovered certain graves contain special collections of objects along with the culture's usual grave goods. These objects might include packets of herbs, tiny weapons, seeds, small figurines, animal teeth or claws, pieces of animal fur or hair, unusually shaped rocks, crystals, beads, bones, or other talismans. These objects, often collected into bundles, are found carefully placed under and around the earthly remains of the interred person. Contemporary archaeologists now define these special burials as shaman graves and the unusual contents found within them to be significant ritual or power objects.

Figure 51. An animal tooth drilled with a hole for hanging on a shaman's costume. (Pen and ink ©2013 Evelyn C. Rysdyk)

A 12,000-year-old grave[31], discovered in 2008, held just such kinds of unusual objects. Along with remains of a forty-five-year-old woman, the Neolithic grave contained fifty tortoise shells, the wing bone of a golden eagle, and various other animal bones and was significantly more intricate than the rest of the community's burials. This discovery is the oldest found to date but very like one uncovered in Bad Dürrenberg, a town in the Saalekreis district, in Saxony-Anhalt, Germany, described as that of

> . . . *a woman who is believed to be a shaman. Her rich set of grave-goods is entirely unusual and mysterious. . . . This 25–35-year-old "special woman", along with a 6- to 12-month-old child, was laid out on a fill of red [soil]. . . . Her burial took place around 9,000–8,600 years ago, isolated in the landscape. The exceptionally rich collection of grave-goods is evidence that the dead woman had a special role in society. A remarkable feature is the enormous variety of animal species present in the grave, which were not all food supplies for the beyond. Ethnographic parallels suggest that many objects may be explained as items used in shamanistic practices.*[32]

Figure 52. Feathers are a part of many shaman bundles. (Pen and ink ©2013 Evelyn C. Rysdyk)

Similar burials of women and also of men have been found in Europe, across Asia, in the Arctic, and throughout the Americas. It seems that the unusual objects, fetishes, and talismans found in these burials not only identify the occupants as shamans, they themselves were also apparently so important to the spirit walker that they needed to accompany them on their final journeys into the spirit world.

This is consistent with the way certain items are regarded by the tribal shamans with whom I have studied. Along with their usual tools such as rattles or drums, each of them had pouches, bags, or bundles of especially sacred, talismanic objects that were a part of their personal attire, featured upon their altars, or deemed essential to their working environment.

Spirit Stand-Ins

Some spirit bundles embody the spirits of the spirit walker's helpers. If dedicated to an animal spirit or bird, these bundles may contain carved representations of the animal and may also include the creature's claws, bones, feathers, or fur. If the bundle represents a human-formed spirit, it might have a picture or small statue along with dried flowers, herbs, crystals, or other offerings. Since, as with all other shamanic power objects, these bundles are inspirited and so considered alive, they are not simple representations but rather actual manifestations of the spirits they honor. As such, they bring the spirit's intangible essence into form, thereby allowing the spirit to interact with the physical plane.

Many different objects may be used as talismans for the spirit walker and can be included in a spirit bundle or pouch. Objects may include those gathered during a powerful experience, given to the spirit walker by an elder or teacher, symbolizing images or spirits encountered in dreams, or be anything else that has a spiritual significance to the spirit walker. These objects may include quartz crystals, special beads, animal claws, feathers, or small figurines.

Figure 53. Crystals are a part of many shaman bundles.

Among the Pueblo peoples of the southwestern United States, there is a tradition of carving small spirit figures in stone, antler, shell, wood, or other natural materials. The Zuni people are especially well known for these fetishes, which may include animal figures as well as images of deities or representations of natural forces. Common animal figures include the bear, hummingbird, snake, coyote, dragonfly, raven, deer, horse, eagle, lizard, wolf, fish, and frog.

Along with the many different animals that might be depicted, a spirit such as the thunderbird would be honored in carvings for its ability to gather clouds and bring the blessing of rain. The Corn Maiden is another common figure as it is she who brings life to the corn plants and therefore nourishment to the Zuni people.

The Inuit people of the Arctic traditionally fashioned small carvings of animals and other helping spirits from walrus ivory and whalebone. These images could be used to bring game animals to the hunters, to honor personal or clan ancestors, or be part of a shaman's protection. Whales, seals, seabirds, and polar bears are the most commonly represented. Interestingly, the Inuit people also carved images of distorted-looking spirits called *tupilak* that look like monsters made from different parts of people and animals. When used for malevolent purposes, images like these could be used to control an evil or disease-causing spirit for the purpose of causing harm.

Figure 54. Haida shaman's carved ivory bear fetish. (Pen and ink ©2013 Evelyn C. Rysdyk)

Shamans from the Pacific Northwest coast of North America wore amulets and figures carved from bone and cedar. Some of these were gathered into necklaces containing many figures. These necklaces were worn in shamanic rituals as spiritual jewelry, to honor the benevolent spirits working with the shaman and for protection.

Himalayan *Gaus*

In the Tibetan Buddhist tradition, small portable prayer boxes made of metal are quite common. These *gaus* hold small spiritual objects, statues of deities, seeds or grains blessed by a lama, sacred relics, or *tsatsas*, prayers or mantras that have been printed on cloth or slips of paper, or anything else the owner wishes.

A *gau* may be made of copper, brass, and tin or even of precious metals such as silver and gold. They range in size from those small enough to be worn on a light chain as a pendant to quite large containers better suited to permanent altars in the home or a ritual space.

Some spirit walkers have adapted these elaborate containers to hold their sacred power objects and wear them during ceremony either around the neck or across the body.

Another Kind of "Bundle"

Some collections of spiritual objects may not be in the form of a bag or pouch. While figurines might be used individually or included in a larger bundle or pouch of power objects, sometimes these talismans have been sewn onto the shaman's ritual clothing, as in the case of Siberian practitioners. In that instance, the effect is to place the spirit walker *inside* of a spirit bundle by literally surrounding the individual with power objects and living representations of spiritual allies.

A glass jar serves as a container for talismans on the healing *mesa*,[33] or altar, of a Peruvian north coast shaman. Called a *seguro del curandera(o)*, this jar is considered the primary talisman of the shamanic healer. It is in this artifact that the spirit walker's power is concentrated. Containing coins, small figures, talismans, symbols of the shaman's protective spirits, sweets, healing herbs, and some of the *curandera* or *curandero*'s own hair or nails, this jar functions as a spiritual alter ego. Set in the central field of the *mesa*, this object can hold the delicate balance of the energies when the healer stands up from her or his central place behind the altar to work on a patient or may be used to re-inspirit the spirit walker if she or he becomes weakened in the course of dealing with a dangerous spirit, such as those that cause serious illnesses.

In the Andes, the spirit walkers, or *paqos*, create bundles of stones or other talismans wrapped in a woven cloth that together function as a portable altar. When the cloth is opened, the objects are arranged in a ceremonial manner that becomes the shaman's map of the cosmos, the ground on which spirit work is performed, and a second home for the spirits that work with the *paqo*. In addition, this *mesa* becomes a kind of "control panel" for balancing spiritual energies to produce harmony. The effect of this balancing generates healing for a people or place. Shamans of the region also may pass a closed *mesa* bundle over a person to effect healing.

Prayer or Offering Bundles

Prayer bundles are also created as offerings to the spirits. The people of Peru, Bolivia, and Ecuador put together elaborate offering bundles that are either burned or buried. These *despachos* are used to thank Mother Earth, Pachamama, for her many gifts and to assure that the bounty she provides will continue to flow. These bundles contain many ingredients, such as sweets, seeds, play money, flowers, and other objects that specifically pertain to the purpose of the offering. For instance, if a person desires to start a business, the *despacho* bundle would have small symbols of the tools necessary for that kind of work. The shaman's markets throughout the region have tiny versions of animals, trucks, tools, houses, cars, and other necessities of life that could be included in a *despacho*.[34]

Exercise: Creating a Spirit Bundle

Before you decide what you would like to include in your spirit bundle, do journeys to your helping spirits to find out what purpose your bundle will be used for. This will help you to determine the size and portability required or the materials you will need to contain the objects. For instance, the bundle may need to be small enough to wear in a leather bag around your neck or large enough to take a central place in your home or on your altar. In that case, a special container may be required.

Ask your helpers what they would prefer you to include in the bundle. Do individual journeys to each of them and honor them with a gratitude offering upon your return.

Gathering the Objects

Take your time in selecting your objects. Make sure that they are gathered in a sacred and legal manner! For instance, if you are told by your spirits to include an eagle talon—which is illegal to own in the United States—you can substitute a carving of a talon that you ask your spirits to empower. No animal needs to be harmed nor laws broken for the purpose of gathering power! This would be contrary to the purpose of a spirit walker. We are meant to negotiate harmony and balance, be generous to the spirits, and be conscientious stewards of the natural world.

Remember that objects will never make you a powerful spirit walker in the same way that possessions cannot make you a powerful person! The purpose of your spirit bundle is to augment your relationship with your spirits. It is the relationships themselves that allow you to experience power.

Once you have gathered your objects, find or make a suitable container to hold them. Think about how you want to use the bundle as you consider the container. Will you need to carry your bundle on your person? In that case, a leather bag might be the best choice. If your spirit bundle will live on your altar, you could use a beautiful box, a basket, or a simple roll of cloth to contain it.

Exercise: Empowering Your Bundle

When you are ready to fully empower your bundle, start by making a gratitude offering to the spirits. Honor the spirits of the directions, your power animal, and your spirit teacher. Enter into a journey and connect with your heart to your power animal. When you feel ready, sing your power song and merge with your power animal here in the Middle World. Pick up the bundle. Journey while holding your bundle to each of the spirits it represents. Thank them and ask them to place some of their energy into the bundle. As each one empowers the bundle, begin singing and dancing with the enlivened bundle. When the process feels complete, offer your thanks and gently return to ordinary reality.

When you have returned to ordinary consciousness, take the time to sit with the experience before recording it in your notebook. Let your heart fill with gratitude for the gifts you have received in this experience and lovingly place an offering on the Earth.

Journey Explorations

- Journey to a teacher or power animal to ask: "What are the ways I am to use this bundle in my shamanic practice?"

Record the content of your journey and your perceptions about what you receive.

- Journey to a teacher or power animal to ask: "What is the best way to care for my spirit bundle?" Make notes on what you receive.

After each journey, make an offering to the spirits.

Process Questions

- As you work with your spirit bundle, notice what changes you observe in your connection with your helping spirits. Take some time to write your impressions of these shifts.

Record your thoughts and feelings in your journal.

CHAPTER 10

Masks

There are several different reasons for wearing a shamanic mask. The mask assists the spirit walker in deepening a trance; it alters the wearer's appearance so that the transformation into a shamanic spiritual ally is deepened; and it assists the spirit walker's helping spirits in more strongly entering this physical realm. More plainly put, wearing a mask while you perform shamanic activities can support a more powerful spirit walker practice. It also can allow your helping spirits to manifest more strongly in your life.

Masks from regions as far flung as the South Pacific, Africa, and North America fall into this category. Since transformation is precisely what the shaman seeks to have happen during the trance, the mask can assist the viewer or patient in understanding the point at which the shaman undergoes this change. It is easier for the other people of the tribe to see the masked shaman as another being—that is, a being who is possessed by a helping spirit. To accomplish this, the masks may be actual representations of the shaman's helping spirits and protector animal, or they may be created to represent images of the human face when entranced. The peoples of the North America's Pacific coast have created fabulous masks of carved and painted wood that are often decorated with fur, hair, leather, bone, shells, and other materials. Even today, there are many very talented carvers in this region keeping this centuries-old art alive.

Figure 55. Tlingit shaman's mask made from carved cedar wood. The mask is painted and decorated with human hair. The eyes of the mask have been inlaid with abalone shell disks. (Pen and ink ©2013 Evelyn C. Rysdyk)

When placed over the face, these wooden masks also have the effect of altering the wearer's voice. Depending on the mask's construction, it can give the voice an echoing, muffled, or even slightly amplified quality. The changing sound contributes to the mask's overall effectiveness in supporting the shaman's transformation.

Another reason for wearing a mask is to assist the shaman in the actual transformation and to help sustain the trance. The fringed masks of Asia certainly fit into this category. These obscure the shaman's view of ordinary reality, camouflaging or shielding it from the spirit walker's sight. Since a limited view of this reality is still available, such masks are particularly effective when the shaman will be dancing and moving around the patient or in any situation when the wearing of a full blindfold would be impractical. These masks may be simple strips of leather, braided yarn, fur strips, or in the case of one of our apprentices, long strands of seed beads. In the latter example, the curtain of beaded fringe is formed in the image of the eyes of the shaman's tutelary spirit. These spirit eyes sway hypnotically as the shaman's head moves.

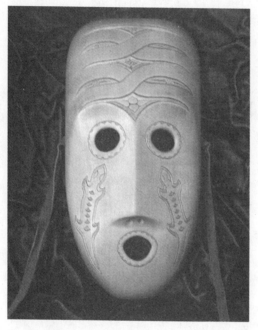

Figure 56. An Ulchi shaman's carved larch wood mask. (Author's photo)

An example of a fur and leather fringe mask is seen in Figure 23 and also the drawing of the Yukaghir shaman in Figure 25. In this example, the strands of the mask are integrated into the shaman's cap. The mask portion consists of a row of cords made from fur and leather twisted together. Each of the individual strands is weighted at the bottom with beads. The strands of this mask are long enough to be tossed over the shoulders when the shaman needs his ordinary vision cleared.

Mongol shamans use a much shorter fringed mask on their headgear. The fringe, which falls just long enough to cover the eyes, is made from black braided wool or cloth meant to represent a woman's bangs, echoing the ancient idea that the first shaman was female. These fringe masks are integrated into the elaborate crowns that these shamans wear. Even a simple piece of cloth may be used like a mask. The 19th-century cultural anthropologist Maria Czaplicka reported in her accounts that the shamans of the Samoyed (now known as Selkup) or Ostyak (now known as the Khant) tribes used such masks. The cloths were held over the face by simple bands around the head.[35]

Exercise: Making Your Own Shamanic Fringe Mask

A fringe mask is an excellent mask for any shamanic practitioner as it is extremely practical. It may be worn in situations when you may also want to see some of your surroundings. This is especially useful if you are dancing as you journey or journeying out in the woods.

The mask explained below consists of three separate elements. These may be constructed from easy-to-cut, soft leather, felt, durable cloth, or another material. Choose your materials after you have completely read through the information below. Allow yourself the freedom to experiment.

Materials and Tools

- A file with pattern and instructions may be downloaded at *www.myspiritwalk.com.*

- Cloth, soft leather, felt, or other materials you decide on after reviewing the three mask elements listed below

- Glue and/or sewing supplies to join the parts

- Paint, beads, or other items to decorate the mask

Make the Fringe Mask

The fringe mask has three parts:

The first piece is a headband strap that is three-quarters of an inch wide and long enough that you can tie it like a lace around your head at the level above your ears. I find that the measurement of the circumference of your head *plus* an additional twenty-four inches is a good length. While this piece can be constructed out of many different materials, it does get quite a bit of wear, especially as the mask needs to be tied tightly enough so it doesn't fall off while you are moving around. For this reason it needs to be the most durable of the three pieces. I prefer using soft leather, although you could use a length of heavy cord, woven upholstery tape, or flat braid from the fabric store.

The second part is the fringe itself. The fringe can be made from a rectangle of soft leather or felt that has been cut into fringe but with the top edge still intact. It can also be individual strands of twisted cord or yarn with beads at the bottom, or put together entirely out of many long strings of beads. Typically, the fringed area of the mask extends from temple to temple and needs to be at least long enough to cover the eyes but can also be made long enough to cover the entire face.

The fringe and the headband strap will need to be joined together. You can glue or sew them together, or punch holes and tie the pieces together. Use whatever method makes sense based upon your materials. If you are unsure about how to proceed, ask for some advice at the craft or fabric store.

The last piece is a decorative forehead band that covers the place where the fringe is connected to the strap. This may be fur, felt, leather, or cloth and could even be painted or beaded if you choose to do so. This piece needs to be long enough to go from one edge of the fringe to the other (temple to temple) and wide enough to cover the area where the fringe and strap are joined together. This is approximately six to seven inches long and about one to two inches wide.

On the day you set aside for making your mask, create sacred space before you begin. Assemble the mask while remaining in a prayerful attitude. Make an offering before you start and after you have completed the mask.

Exercise: Empowering Your Fringe Mask

At this point, your new shaman's fringe mask needs to be enlivened and empowered for its sacred purpose. When you are ready to dedicate your new mask, make a gratitude offering to the spirits. Call with your heart to bring your power animal to you. Give thanks to the spirits and the natural world for your connections with spiritual power. Place the mask over your face and begin a journey to your spirit teacher. Shake your rattle, ring your bell, or play your drum to accompany your journey. Dance and sing to thank this spirit who has chosen to meet with you.

Once you are with your spirit teacher, ask to be merged with your teacher to empower the mask. Allow the teacher to bless it for sacred work.

When the process feels complete, thank the spirits and begin shaking your rattle or bell or drumming to the rhythm of the journey callback signal. Fully unmerge from your spirit teacher and return yourself to ordinary reality.

Upon your return, take ample time to sit with the experience prior to recording it in your notebook. Remember to go outside and make an offering of thanks. Let your heart fill with gratitude for the gifts you have received in this experience and place an offering on the Earth with reverence.

Process Questions

Once the mask is empowered, practice journeying while wearing the mask and standing or moving around in a safe area. Notice how your connection to spirit shifts when you are able to move around while remaining in the shamanic state of consciousness. After some practice, ask yourself the following questions and record what you realize about your own process.

- How does being able to move while journeying alter your experience of the spirit worlds?

- How does wearing your mask change your experience of ordinary reality? Record what you observe about your process.

Exercise: Making a Nature Spirit Mask

One way of honoring the Middle World nature spirits is by making masks to represent them. The following instructions will be for a Green Man mask specifically, but they can be followed as a framework for constructing a mask for any other transcendent Middle World spirit. Instead of silk leaves, you could use fur, twigs, bark, small shells, feathers, or any number of objects that recall the energy of the spirits you have met in your journeys.

Materials and Tools

- Small half-face mask (Such masquerade masks are available at costume or craft stores in a variety of colors. Choose a color that will blend with your materials. Ready-made masks are made of stiffened fabric or papier-mâché. I prefer the fabric, though papier-mâché works equally well.)

Fgure 58. Nature spirit mask (Photo and mask: Heather Harden)

- Silk-like leaves and flowers (available at most craft stores)

- Scissors

- Wire cutters

- Glue gun and glue sticks (*Safety Note:* A glue gun gets hot enough to burn your fingers and mar your work surface. Always rest the glue gun on a heat-resistant surface and use toothpicks or skewers to place tiny items on the mask. Also protect your work surface from stray globs of glue by covering it with several layers of newspaper.)

- Plate or scrap of wood to rest the hot glue gun on

- Toothpicks or bamboo skewers

- Decorative embellishments such as beads, fabric, clean sticks, yarn, and feathers (*Safety Note:* If using feathers found outdoors, place them in a plastic bag and microwave them for ten seconds to kill any feather mites.)

Make the Mask

1. On the day that you plan to make your mask, gather your tools and perform an offering to thank all the spirits.

2. Begin your work by preparing the silk leaves, flowers, and any other embellishments that you have gathered. Remove the leaves and flowers from the larger stems using wire cutters. Trim all small connecting stems as needed. It is helpful to have leaves in a variety of color, shapes, and sizes.

3. Your half-face mask will have a small piece of elastic to hold it on the face. When it is manufactured, the elastic is inserted in the small holes from the outside of the mask and knotted on the inside. The mask will fit more comfortably if the elastic is reversed. Untie the knots and insert the elastic from the back of the mask and retie the knots on the front of the mask. These knots will eventually be hidden by the layers of leaves and flowers you will be gluing on in the next steps.

4. Before you begin gluing anything to the mask, lay it on a flat surface and arrange the leaves and flowers across it until you find an arrangement that pleases you. Start by arranging the larger leaves around the outside edge of the mask. To make the mask bilaterally symmetrical, like your own face, use the same number of leaves of a similar shape and size on the right and left sides of the mask.

5. Once you have the leaves around the outside edge laid out in the pattern you prefer, glue them in place by applying a small to medium dot of glue to the base of the leaf and pressing it firmly onto the mask.

6. Overlap layers of smaller leaves like shingles on a roof to fill in around the eyes and nose, trim the leaves if necessary

to make them fit better. Remember to leave the eye area unobstructed.

7. Continue layering the leaves on the mask until the entire surface is covered. Use a variety of shapes, sizes, and colors to add interest.

8. Once you are satisfied with the foundation of the mask, it is time to put on your embellishments. These can be clusters of small flowers, feathers, single blossoms, small pinecones, or even glitter. Let your work with the spirits guide you in your selections.

9. As with applying the leaves, experiment with the placement of the finishing touches before applying enough glue to the back of the item and pressing it firmly into place on the mask.

As you can see, these masks are fairly easy to make, and you may get inspired to make a few of them. For instance, you may make a different nature spirit mask for each season. Alternately, you may wish to honor all of the different transcendent nature spirits you are meeting with their own mask.

Exercise: Empowering Your Nature Spirit Mask

At this point, your nature spirit mask needs to be enlivened and empowered for its sacred purpose.

1. When you are ready to dedicate your new mask, make a gratitude offering to the spirits. Call with your heart to bring your power animal to you. Give thanks for your connections to the world of spiritual power.

2. When you feel ready, merge with your power animal and begin to dance with your rattle as accompaniment. Place the mask over your face and call the Middle World spirit who is represented in your mask to join you. Shake the rattle, dance, and sing to thank this spirit who has chosen to meet with you.

3. When the process feels complete, shake your rattle to the rhythm of the journey callback signal, thank the Middle World spirit, unmerge from your power animal, and return yourself to ordinary reality.

Upon your return, take ample time to sit with the experience prior to recording it in your notebook. Remember to go outside and make an offering of thanks. Let your heart fill with gratitude for the gifts you have received in this experience and place your offering on the Earth with reverence.

Journey Explorations

- Journey to a teacher or power animal to ask: "What are the ways I am to use this nature spirit mask in my shamanic practice?" Record the content of your journey and your perceptions about what you receive.

- Journey to a teacher or power animal to ask: "What is the best way to care for my nature spirit mask's spirit?" Make notes on what you receive.

- Journey to a teacher or power animal to ask: "What are the appropriate times for me to wear my nature spirit mask?"

After each journey, remember to honor the spirits with an offering.

Process Questions

- As you work with your masks, notice how your connection with your helping spirits may have changed. Take some time to write your impressions of these shifts.

- Notice if you experience different sensations when you are masked. Does your connection to the spirits feel stronger? Record your thoughts and feelings in your journal.

CHAPTER 11

Shamanic Mirrors

In some cultures, shamans wear polished metal disks on the front and sometimes on the back of their costume. This reflects negativity and amplifies access to the positive energy the shaman seeks for a working. Mirrors have been used in this fashion all across Asia from Siberia to China into the Himalayas and down into the foothills of Nepal and northern India.

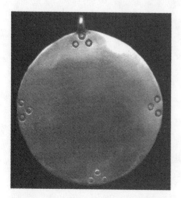

Figure 58. Himalayan shaman's mirror, or *melong*. (Author's photo)

In Asia, many shamans still wear at least one mirror that is sometimes just suspended on a cord and worn around the neck. Such is the case with Bhola Banstola, who wears a small shaman's mirror—known in Tibetan as a *melong*—as a part of his dress. Depending upon the region, shaman's mirrors are of different sizes and have different names.[36] Another form used in Nepal is the *lokur chuni*, a cast metal disk of brass, bronze, or silver, which is polished on one side like a *melong* and has a complex design of protective symbols on the reverse. This can be worn around the neck, sewn onto a coat, or strung inside of a frame drum.

Figure 59. The *lokur chuni* is not only used by shamans in the Himalayas, but also by mothers to protect their children. (Author's photo)

When I visited Nepal recently, I was blessed with the opportunity to observe and receive a healing from the last living Tibetan shaman, or *lhapa*, Nyima Dhondup. As a part of his shamanic costume, he wore around his neck a *melong* nearly seven inches in diameter that had been threaded on a silk scarf. When he prepared to perform healings, he also arranged three slightly smaller *melongs* on his altar. These were placed upright in bowls that had been piled high with grain or flour as mounds to represent the healing mountains from which the shaman received power. Just behind the *melongs* were images of Nyima's healing deities. The *melongs* functioned as temporary houses for these powerful spirits. When he was healing people, the deities entered the room from these mirrors to work with him. Other Himalayan shamans use a *melong* in a similar fashion. Bhola's altar always has a large *melong* which functions as a portal through which beneficial spirits may enter the room for healing as well as for his personal protection.

Mirrors can also be tools for divination. Gazing into a reflective or luminous surface to receive spiritual information is called scrying. Using inner sight, a shaman may perceive the illness afflicting a patient or search for lost objects and errant souls. Crystals, pools of water, or mirrors may all be used for this purpose. As with all of the shaman's empowered regalia, a mirror may be used to heal when the energies stored in it are transferred to whatever or whoever requires the shaman's help.

Exercise: Making a Shaman's Mirror

Although there are some shaman's mirrors and *melongs* being offered on the Internet, it is also possible to make a simple shaman's mirror from a disk of copper or brass. Small brass disks sold as key tags can be purchased from the hardware store, and larger ones can be secured from companies that supply metal workers. A disk about four inches across works beautifully on a costume, while smaller disks make excellent protective amulets.

Materials and Tools

- Copper or brass disk

- Drill and eighth-inch drill bit

- Round file

- Wadding polish such as Nevr-Dull or another metal polish

- Cord to wear the disk or thread to secure it to a costume

- Electric engraver to place designs into the metal (optional)

Make the Mirror

Take the disk you have chosen and drill a hole that will allow it to be either sewn to your costume or strung as an amulet. When that is completed, file the hole smooth with a round file and then use a metal polish to shine it to a brilliant finish.

When you are done, follow this by having your spirit teacher empower the mirror for your shamanic work as you have done with other sacred objects.

Journey Explorations

- Journey to a teacher or power animal to ask: "What are the ways I am to use this mirror in my shamanic practice?"

Record the content of your journey and your perceptions about what you receive.

Process Questions

- As you work with your shaman's mirror, what are the feelings you experience?

- Under what circumstances do you feel called to use it?

Record your impressions.

CHAPTER 12

Spirit Figures

There seems to be an ancient need we humans fulfill by representing spirits in tangible form. We use objects and especially humanlike figures to bridge the visible and invisible worlds—to help bring the intangible worlds here. In this way, we keep our protector spirits and beloved ancestral spirits close to us so that we can receive their blessings.

Making spirit figures also seems to be a nearly universal shamanic custom. Shamanic spirit figures are so widespread that examples may be found from as diverse cultures as those of Papua New Guinea, Micronesia, Asia, the Arctic, Africa, and both North and South America. These figures often are the shaman's helper spirits and may embody ancestors, an animal, a bird, or hybridized animal-bird human forms. They are enlivened by the shaman and so become actual helpers in the shaman's work. They may serve as a protector, healer, or guide to the shaman or may be given to a patient to effect a healing. Larger figures may be placed in the landscape, the house, or a healing place. Smaller figures may be sewn on a shaman's coat, hung inside a drum, worn around the neck, or carried in small pouches in the manner of the Native American fetishes found among the peoples of the southwestern United States.

Figure 60. This small Ulchi *saiven* is a healing amulet. It may be placed around a person's neck to protect and restore the wearer. The *saiven* is carved from larch, the most sacred tree of the Ulchi people. (Pen and ink drawing ©2013 Evelyn C. Rysdyk. Private collection.)

Ulchi carvings of *saivens* are excellent examples of this kind of practice. I was first exposed to this work when my partner Allie and I worked with Grandfather Misha. In his culture, spirit figures are a prevalent part of the spiritual landscape. Along with figures representing the ancestors, *saivens* are used as protectors in the house, on the exterior of the house, or out on the land. These figures represent a local nature spirit and are worn for healing and used by shamans in their work.

Depending on what sort of healing is necessary for a patient, the Ulchi shaman would meet with spirits to prescribe a small carving of a *saiven* or spirit helper. Once created by the carver in the village, the shaman would imbue the statue with the essence of the spirit represented by the object. Typically, the spirit figure directly delivers healing energy to the patient by being worn close to the body. The psychological benefit of having a concrete reminder of the process also contributes to the depth of the healing the patient receives. Using wooden effigies in this fashion has the effect of engaging the patient's own spirit in the healing process, thereby amplifying the spiritual work done on his or her behalf. This method is so successful among the Ulchi that there are a wide variety of effigies that may be prescribed. Due to this remarkable diversity, healing *saivens* may be used to treat maladies as diverse as depression, intestinal pain, poor hearing, or simple bad luck.

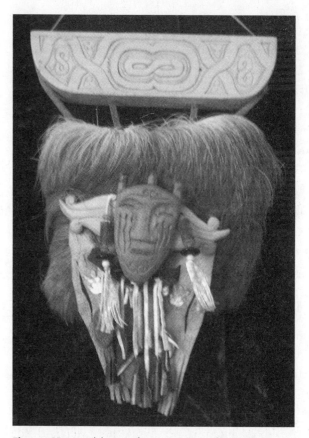

Figure 61. An Ulchi spirit figure, or *saiven*, for protecting a space used for healing work. The carving represents the shaman surrounded by his spiritual allies or ancestors. (Private collection. Author's photo)

When Grandfather Misha traveled to the United States, he brought several small figures that had been carved in his village. We purchased two of these figures, one of which was for illnesses/maladies of the belly. This little, bear-shaped effigy has a large, square section cut out of its abdomen and was made to be worn close to the body. This act of "wounding" or removing a portion of a wooden spirit figure—widespread across Siberia—is done so that the spirit of the effigy takes on the illness, thereby removing it from the patient. It reveals the shamanic belief that illnesses have their own spirits that require a "home."

In keeping with Ulchi traditions, a *saiven* statue is seen as alive and therefore must be fed to keep the spirit held inside it strong. This ensures that the spirit will continue its protective and healing duties. This is also a common practice among the Pueblo peoples of North America. When either a kachina figure or fetish carving has been imbued with a spirit for ritual purposes, it also needs to be fed in some manner, most often with cornmeal or tobacco. This ritual feeding supports the patient's relationship with the healing spirits. In making offerings of food, the patient shows gratitude and stays engaged with the healing process. This act may also be seen as a kind of transference of the responsibility for continued healing from the healer to the patient. By taking on caring for the spirit inside the *saiven*, the patient is in essence caring for his/her *own* spirit by proxy.

In the Amur River region, the homeland of the Ulchi and Nanai people, there is a story that tells how *saivens* were once raised into an army to avenge wrongdoing. In the story, a young man returns home from hunting to find invaders have murdered all the people of his village. In his grief, he carves and empowers a large group of human-size effigies. He then sets this army on the marauders. When they have completed their gruesome duty, he uses his ax to remove their faces so they are once again just simple logs. The young man then lashes these logs together to take him farther down the Amur River and hopefully into a new life.[37]

When Ai Churek traveled from her home in Tuva to our home in Maine, she brought a full complement of spirit effigies in her luggage. Most of them were made from cloth and leather. These doll-like figures represented the spirits that support the shaman's work and included representations of the shaman's ancestors. These images were called upon to both bring the shaman power as well as to actually implement the work of healing. Some of Ai Churek's personal effigies were sewn to a small cloth and had been passed down from her mother, who had also been a shaman. Ai Churek's mother had, in turn, received them from her shaman mother. For Ai Churek, these figures had a great deal of power, as they were well over a hundred years old and held the collected energy of generations of her shaman ancestors.

Exercise: Creating a Spirit Figure

As a spirit walker, you may choose to keep figures that represent and hold the energies of your helper spirits. If you do, there are easy ways to fashion simple figures that can be very powerful. Adding eyes and a nose to a short stick with paint or a permanent marking pen is a way to create the simplest figure. I find that the act of adding eyes to anything has the effect of making any "it" into a "she" or "he."

A slightly more elaborate spirit figure may be made with a small forked branch and smaller straight stick. If you hold a forked stick with the fork facing downward, you can easily see legs and a torso. If you lash a second stick perpendicular to the first and a little way down from the top, you have arms. A simple figure like this functions as the handle of one of my drums.

Figure 62. Siberian-style spirit figure made from lightning-struck maple used as a frame drum handle. (Private collection. Author's photo)

It is easy to see how, with some heavy thread or cord and a pile of carefully chosen sticks, you could craft a bunch of simple spirit figures in a very short time. If this is appealing, try also making simple animal figures to honor your power animal. In either case, remember that you will decorate these figures. This is done in accordance with the information you will receive in journeys to your helping spirits.

If you have crafting skills, you could carve a more detailed figure from wood, and if you sew, you might want to construct cloth figures. Images made from clay can also be very effective for those of you who work with pottery. Let your heart and imagination help you to make something that is just right.

When you have completed your figure to your liking, follow the steps you have taken before to empower the figure and make an offering to thank the spirits for their participation in your work.

Journey Explorations

- Journey to a teacher or power animal to ask: "How should I decorate this spirit figure?"

- Journey to a teacher or power animal to ask: "What are the ways I am to use this spirit figure in my shamanic practice?" Record the content of your journey and your perceptions about what you receive.

- Journey to a teacher or power animal to ask: "What is the best way to care for my spirit figure?"

After each journey, remember to make an offering to the spirits.

Process Questions

- What was it like to make and empower a spirit figure?

Record what you have noticed.

CHAPTER 13

Feathers and Fans

M any shamans use feathers as a part of their paraphernalia. A single feather may be applied to many purposes. A feather may be a talisman that represents a shaman's helping spirit. A feather may also be a simple fan for smudging, a ritual of fumigating with an herbal smoke for healing, clearing, or blessing. This is a common shamanic practice that may be performed prior to engaging in any journeying or ritual work. Smudging can effect different changes in the space, all of which are based upon a shaman's intent. Blessing with smoke can remove unbeneficial influences from an area in which you are planning to do spiritual work. Fragrant smoke can also enliven a space by uplifting the energy. There are some helping spirits that enjoy being fed with smoke as well. In some cases, smoke itself may be a part of a healing ceremony when used by the shaman to cleanse a patient of intrusive energy.

In North America, the most common plant for smudging is dried sage. Two varieties of this plant, white sage and desert sage, are turned to for this purpose. Even ordinary people have taken to using their smoke to clear a space of "negative" energy. The plants are burned either as loose leaves in a vessel such as an abalone shell or as a bundle known commonly as a smudge stick or smudge wand.

Figure 63. Prayer feather with a bead-wrapped quill handle. (Pen and ink ©2013 Evelyn C. Rysdyk)

In Siberia, among the Ulchi people, the smoke from burning *senkure* leaves purifies the space in which the healing ceremony, or *kamlanie*, will be performed. This same plant is used to charge and purify water on the shaman's altar as well as that ingested by the shaman him or herself during the *undee* processional ritual that precedes the actual healing ceremony.[38] While each culture uses a different plant for this work, those most commonly utilized in the Americas are sage, sweetgrass, cedar, copal resin, *palo santo* wood, and tobacco.

If you are called to use a feather in your practice, it is important to know that some critical legal limitations exist. The United States government has very strict and highly specific laws restricting the ownership and use of certain bird and animal products. Before you do anything with any animal or bird remains or feathers, please consult the U.S. Fish and Wildlife Service office in your area to prevent serious legal problems. These laws were put in place to prevent the destruction of wildlife and therefore must be obeyed by anyone on the shamanic path.

In general, those animals or birds that are legally hunted in your area may be used for sacred or craft purposes. Usual examples are turkey, partridge, grouse, Canada goose, crow, and some ducks. Feathers from domesticated birds may also be used safely. Absolutely no songbird, raptor, or other waterfowl feathers are legal to own. This holds true even if you found the feather on the ground by your bird feeder, in the woods, or on the beach! A

$1,500 fine can be levied on you by the U.S. government for each illegal feather that you have in your possession.

Once you have secured a legal feather, you will need to keep it in a safe place. The container must be rigid to protect from breakage as well as closed to keep out clothes moths whose larvae delight in munching on feathers.

Sometimes a single feather may not be enough to serve a shaman's purpose. In these cases a fan of several feathers or even an entire bird wing may be called for.

Figure 64. Feather fan by the Penobscot healer Roger Nighthawk. This fan is made from feathers that have been secured with leather to the jawbone of a deer. It is used in a healing ceremony to sweep away intrusive energy and negative influences from a patient. (Private collection. Pen and ink ©2013 Evelyn C. Rysdyk)

Some of the finest examples of shamanic fans are found among the indigenous peoples of the Americas. Fans may be of two general types—either flat with feathers that are fixed in place or those with feathers that have been secured on strips of leather so that they may loosely fly around when the fan is shaken. It is the former style of fan that is more commonly utilized in an individual shamanic healing ceremony. The latter type, most often seen during Native American Church ceremonies, is sometimes referred to as a peyote fan. Fans may be created with the brightly colored feathers of domestic parrot or macaws. Sometimes different kinds, sizes, and colors of feathers are combined in the same fan. The entire handle surface can often be quite lavishly decorated with very colorful beadwork.

Flat fans are usually created by mounting either individual feathers or a preserved bird's wing or a bird's tail feathers to a handle. When individual feathers are used, they are mounted spread out to better resemble a wing. Handle materials range from wood that has been decorated with cloth, leather, and/or beads to bones such as half of a jawbone. Some fans just terminate in a simple cord or braided leather thong which functions as a handle.

Exercise: Preparing a Bird Wing to Make a Fan

I have included this section for educational purposes. Please thoroughly read through the entire section before attempting to secure an appropriately legal bird carcass and prepare its wing.

Materials and Tools

- A freshly killed, legal bird carcass

- A sharp knife

- Rubber gloves

- A filter mask

- Plastic bags for safe disposal

- A box big enough to contain an extended wing from the bird

- A piece of stiff cardboard or foam core board that is large enough to support the extended wing and also lie flat inside the bottom of the box

- A large needle and heavy thread

- Disinfectant such as chlorine bleach

- Borax powder

Make the Fan

To make a fan from a legal bird's wing or tail feathers, it is best to start with a very freshly killed bird. Once rigor mortis occurs, the wing will not be able to extend into a fan and so the carcass will be useless. Additionally, as a body begins to decay and the flesh changes—which starts immediately after death—it becomes pretty untenable to use the bird's body for sacred purpose. The strong odors of decomposition are nearly impossible to get out of the feathers. Even if it is only hours old, it is still critical to remember that harvesting from a dead body is very dangerous. *Always* use good rubber gloves and a filter mask to protect yourself from bacteriological hazards. For this and obvious odor issues, it is best to do this kind of work outdoors.

When you are through, it is also critical to thoroughly wash and disinfect any surfaces that the dead creature came into contact with using a chorine bleach solution of three-quarters of a cup of bleach to one gallon of water. *(Follow all recommended cautions when using chlorine beach or other* disinfectants.) Any parts of the dead animal or bird that are thrown into the trash must be double-bagged in plastic to protect others. Your life, the lives of other people, and the lives of your pets depend on it!

While wearing gloves, carefully cut through the flesh where the wing meets the body using a sharp knife. (You will need to be able to properly disinfect this knife as well!) As you wiggle the wing around, you will notice that there is a bone that extends into the chest. You'll want to keep that bone connected to the wing when you remove it. This will eventually be part of the handle of your fan. Once the wing is free from the body, set it aside and properly dispose of the rest of the body.

Now, pick up your stiff piece of cardboard or artist's foam core board. Spread the wing open and either pin it or stitch it to the cardboard with the outside of the wing touching the cardboard; in other words, the inside of the wing faces up. Don't force the wing open, just allow it to open at a natural angle. The cardboard should be large enough to completely support the entire wing. Then set this cardboard with the attached wing inside your box to contain the mess that follows later.

Carefully wash all your tools, knives, etc., in the chlorine bleach solution. The gloves can be tossed away with the body.

Now it is time to *completely* cover the entire wing, which has been set into the box, with borax powder. Borax powder is available in the detergent aisle of the supermarket. *Only borax will work for this process!*

Pay special attention to covering all the exposed flesh. Borax acts as an antibacterial as well as a desiccating agent. Place the box in a cool, dry place for about two months. The top of a closet works well for this, or you may want to put the box on a shelf in the garage. Cellars are not a good choice as they are usually too damp. As the flesh shrinks, it will tighten around the bones making the fan rigid in the shape in which it was attached to the cardboard. After two months, dispose of the borax by pouring it into a double-bagged trash container, and gently free the wing from the cardboard.

Smooth out any ruffled feathers. The handle bone may now be wrapped with cloth or leather and decorated.

Store the finished fan in a sturdy box with cedar shavings. These are easily purchased at pet supply shops, as hamster bedding. The cedar shavings will keep the fan safe from the ravages of clothes moth larvae. I know from experience that these insects enjoy feathers even more than wool. They can quickly devour the body of a feather, leaving a ruined lacework in its place. A bit of prevention for your fan will be well worth the effort.

Journey Explorations

- Journey with your power animal or teacher to meet the bird who gave you part of its body. Ask it what its spirit would like in return for the gift of the feather or wing. (At the very least, do a gratitude ceremony for the gift.)

- Journey to a teacher or power animal to ask: "At what times am I to use my feather or fan?"

- Journey to a teacher or power animal to ask: "How is this feather or fan to be decorated?"

- Journey to a teacher or power animal to ask: "How do I care for this feather or fan?"

Record the content of each journey and your perceptions about what you receive.

Process Questions

- Articulate, as best as you can, in your journal, the bodily, emotional, and spiritual sensations of working with the bird energy present in your feather or fan.

- How has your perception shifted about this species of bird? Record what you notice.

- As you work with your feather or fan, keep aware of the shifts and changes you experience. Are you more drawn to use the feather or fan for clearing space, centering yourself during your own prayers, or for some other purpose?

Keep notes on how your process shifts and changes.

CHAPTER 14

Wands and *Phurbas*

Wands, or *phurbas*, are tools that a shaman may use to magnify intentions and to conduct spiritual energy. Although lightning may never shoot from your implement as shown in movies about young wizards, the idea is still the same. A wand, or *phurba*, becomes an extension of the shaman's body, and on occasion through regular use, it may also transmit power on its own.

Curanderos' Mesas

An excellent example of this may be found among the shamans of the Peruvian north coast who have wands and short staffs as implements on their *mesa*, or altar. When used in a healing ceremony, these wands are arranged in an upright row at the head of the ceremonial altar along with swords or long knives. Holding the energy of each of the shaman's many *compadres*—helpful and healing spirits—these implements range from about one to three feet long. During the ceremony, the various wands—each one living and filled with spirit—are used to cleanse the patient of negative energy, the spirits of sickness, and bad luck. Many of these short staffs are made from a very dense, dark, Amazonian wood (*Geonoma weberbaueri*, known in Spanish as *chonta-duro*). They are carved at the top with figures of the particular spirits and saints that the wands embody. Not only are the images sacred, but also the wood itself comes from a highly sacred tree of the region. This species of palm from the upper Amazon grows at a higher elevation than any other palm tree, and the native people, such as the Shuar of Ecuador, see this as their Tree of Life. This may stem from the fact that objects created from this *chonta-duro* seem to be everlasting in that the wood doesn't decay, even though it is subjected to constant, tropical dampness. Other wood either rots or sprouts in these conditions.

Figure 65. Contemporary shaman's *mesa* in the style of the Peruvian north coast, simplified for traveling. (Author's photo)

Indeed, for sheer amount of paraphernalia, the *curanderos* of the Peruvian north coast take the prize. These shamans' large *mesas*, or healing altars, are set with an extraordinary range of implements. They may include objects as diverse as swords, statues of saints, perfume, bones, pottery, crucifixes, preserved fish, jars of herbs, archaeological finds, and other quite unusual elements. The altar of the famous Peruvian *curandero* Don Eduardo Calderón Palomino held well over eighty different objects.[39]

The *Phurba*

The *phurba* or *kilaya* (Sanskrit) is a ritual implement that is common to Tibetan Buddhist practices, Bon traditional rituals, and Himalayan shamanic practices. Among shamans, the *phurba* may be seen as a representation of the *axis mundi*, or World Tree. This central column of the cosmos unites the realms of the Upper, Middle, and Lower Worlds. In addition, it functions as the hub for the cardinal directions, the wheel of existence, and the still point around which the stars move. In essence, it represents that which unites and holds the cosmos together. It provides a counterbalance to the forces of chaos that are simultaneously pulling the cosmos apart into its constituent components. In this way, the *phurba* is similar to the shaman's staff and to the center of the Peruvian shaman's *mesa*.

Attending to this balance in the human world, shamans use the *phurba* as a stake to anchor themselves to the center of All Worlds as they engage with the forces of chaos and disease. It is common in Himalayan shamanic traditions to stand the *phurba* vertically, point down into a basket or bowl of rice or other soft grain if the *phurba* is wooden, or into a stand or the ground if it is metal. In this position, the *phurba* provides stability on the altar or ceremonial space. In the Himalayan traditions, only those initiated in its use, or otherwise empowered, may wield it. The *phurba* affixes the energies of the heavens to the Earth, thereby establishing energetic continuity and balanced flow. Working in this way, the *phurba* unites energies that have been torn apart, dislocated, or dissociated.

Figure 66. A wooden shaman's *phurba* from Nepal. (Pen and ink ©2013 Evelyn C. Rysdyk)

In a healing, the *phurba* can be used to gather negative spiritual energy as one might gather wool on a spindle. This gathered energy is then staked into the ground so that the negative influences are themselves anchored to the earth where they can be transmuted. The *phurba* thus functions like the sacred mountains of the Himalayas, which folk traditions liken to great pegs that hold the Earth itself together.

The *phurba* may be seen as a representation of the Buddhist deity Dorje Phurba, also known as Vajrakilaya, who embodies the enlightened activity of all the Buddhas. This wrathful deity is able to remove obstacles, destroy the forces hostile to compassion, and purify spiritual pollution. The working shaman becomes a manifestation of Dorje Phurba—moving through the realms to defeat chaos and disease while bringing harmony. In essence, the *phurba* and shaman become one entity.

For the shaman to accomplish this, the *phurba* must first be consecrated to this task and bound with strips of sacred cloth or with rainbow threads. It is used by the shaman to cure disease, perform extraction, conduct exorcism, defeat negative influences on a person or place, sanctify food or drink, assist in meditation, and tether the shaman so that she or he may safely return to this reality.

In the hands of a shaman, the *phurba* augments intent. Along with healing an individual, a *phurba* can assist the shaman in clearing a space of harmful entities. Following a shaman's intent, a *phurba* can also sanctify a drink or healing potion on behalf of a patient when the tip of the blade is placed into the liquid—thereby removing any unbeneficial energy and making it spiritually pure. The pommel of the *phurba* can also impart a blessing or calming influence upon an overly excited patient or calm a space's energy. Patients who are dissociated or ungrounded may be told to hold the *phurba* or may have the *phurba* lain on their prone body, aligned with their midline to organize and harmonize their energy system. As is the case with every shaman's tool, the *phurba* is a living entity whose applications can shift and change based upon immediate circumstances and the needs or intent of the shaman who wields it.

Made of iron, copper, clay, bone, horn, crystal, or wood (usually wild juniper, which is purported to have holy properties), the *phurba* is a unique dagger having three distinct sections: a pommel, a handle, and a blade. These sections may be seen to represent specific elements or features:

	Pommel	Handle	Blade
Human Body	Head	Torso	Legs
Shamanic Universe	Upper World	Middle World	Lower World
Physical Direction	West	Center	East
Temporal Direction	Past	Present	Future
Gender Energies	Male	Neutral	Female
Planetary Aspects	Sky	Earth	Waters

As well as embodying the triune nature of the universe, this triple aspect reflects the *phurba*'s power to transmute the three negative energies known variously as attachment/craving/desire, delusion/ignorance/misconception, and aversion/fear/hate. Three is also sacred to the primary god of the Hindu religion, Shiva, who is also honored by Himalayan shamans.

To represent all of the above energies, the *phurba* has different thematic representations in each of its three segments. Every individual *phurba* is also unique and so has its own combination of images. What follows is an explanation of imagery that may be present on the *phurba*. This will help you to choose the perfect *phurba* for your spirit walker tool kit.

Pommel—Head—of the *Phurba*

A Nepalese shamanic *phurba* has various protective, healing, or harmony-producing representations on its pommel. As such the top end of the *phurba* may be used to impart a blessing on a person, place, or object.

Vajrakilaya or **Dorje Phurba** is the Himalayan deity of purification. This entity is usually shown in three forms or with three faces—one joyful, one peaceful, and one wrathful. In Buddhism, these three faces represent the many aspects of compassion.

The **umbrella** is one of the eight auspicious symbols of Tibetan Buddhism. This image represents protection from harmful forces and illness as well as the expansiveness and unfolding of space/heaven. It is an image of protection.

The **sacred mushroom cap** represents the sacred medicinal mushrooms used by Himalayan shamans. In this way, the mushroom stands as an allegory for both vision and healing.

The **horse's head** is a representation of the wind horse, which has its origins in the shamanic traditions of central Asia. It is an allegory for the human soul—the part of the shaman that can travel through the realms—and also a force that assists in creating order and harmony. Mongolian legends report a magical horse, which was born as a foal with eight legs and the ability to fly—an interesting parallel to Odin's eight-legged flying steed Sleipnir. This wind horse was the spiritual child of a shaman woman, and it helped her to escape the clutches of an evil ruler. In Tibetan Buddhist traditions, the wind horse's appearance is supposed to bring peace, wealth, and harmony.

A horse's head may also refer to Hayagriva, a Buddhist bodhisattva or fully enlightened being. He is depicted with a human body and a horse's head or as a wrathful face with a horse's head above. He represents the triumph of pure divine wisdom. His blessings are sought when beginning study of both sacred and secular subjects.

The **monkey** image is an early form for Buddha as well as Hanuman, the Hindu god who lifted mountains and whose energy is said to remove the fear of demons.

The **snow lion** represents unconditional cheerfulness and a mind that is clear and precise. Its main qualities are fearlessness and holding the energies of the sacred mountain elevations.

The *chorten* or *stupa* is a reliquary for a saint's bones or relics or a Buddhist shrine. In Nepali shamanic traditions, this image correlates with the symbolism of the Kalachakra symbol that protects the bearer against negative influences.

The **guardian or ancestor** is similar to the wooden guardian cult figures found on houses in Nepal. Holding the *Namaste* gesture of prayer, this figure reminds us of the divinity that we all carry as well as the Oneness to which all life belongs.

Ganesha is a Hindu deity with an elephant's head who is also honored by Buddhists as Ganapati, a powerful worldly protector, as well as by shamans. Ganesha is the Remover of Obstacles, Insurer of Success, and Lord of Beginnings. He also puts up beneficial obstacles to impede negative forces. It is said that Ganesha holds the cosmic eggs of past, present, and future inside his belly and that he is a representation of *OM*, the seed syllable of creation. He is sometimes portrayed beside the Mahakala or wrathful form of Buddha.

Bird forms are especially seen on *phurbas* belonging to the shamans of the mid-west hill tribes in Nepal. They represent the energies of air and the above or Upper World direction.

Handle—Middle—of the *Phurba*

The *vajra* symbol is often at the core of the *phurba*'s handle, representing the incorruptible, diamond lightning bolt. It can cut any substance but not itself be cut and is therefore an irresistible force. It represents the flash of insight, the firmness of spirit, and spiritual power.

This *vajra* or *dorje* also has three parts, echoing the triune nature of the *phurba*. The *vajra* or *dorje* is also implied through the representations of either knot work or two lotus blossoms on either side of a sphere. This image invests the energy of the *phurba* with the symbolic nature of a diamond's indestructibility and that of the irresistible force of the thunderbolt. This image is believed to represent firmness of spirit and spiritual power.

The **trident** or *trisul* represents the powers of Shiva—primary god of the Hindu religion—who is often the protector of Himalayan shamans. The sacred number three is represented again here, as well.

Blade—Bottom—of the *Phurba*

Repeating the triune theme, the blade of a *phurba* has a triangular, three-sided point. As it is the end of the implement that emanates power, it sometimes originates with the mouth of a fierce being. This may be a wrathful aspect of Ganesha/ Ganapati, insuring the success of the healer; the sea monster Makara, who is associated with the Lower World; or a Garuda, a being that defeats the disease-causing serpent spirits.

In addition, since the blade is preceded by the vajra, it emanates that protective and harmonious energy, as well.

Makara has a fish body with an elephant's head. Tradition identifies Makara with water, the source of all existence and fertility.

Nagas are snake nature spirits and the protectors of springs, wells, and rivers and as such are guardians of treasure. They bring rain, and thus fertility, but are also thought to bring disasters such as floods, sickness, and drought. The nagas on a *phurba* are under the influence of the being just above them and are therefore benevolent in nature. Shown entwined, they are working on behalf of harmony, fertility, and creation and in this form are reminiscent of the Staff of Asclepius and the Caduceus of Hermes.

Garuda is a protective entity represented in Hindu, Buddhist, and Bon traditions. It is a mythical, semidivine bird-like creature that is the enemy of the serpent spirits or nagas. Garuda is typically invoked in order to counter illnesses provoked by negative naga spirits.

Whichever being is represented, the blade's origin in its mouth implies that it is the "voice" or power of the deity manifesting in the world—in other words, its protective energy in action.

Choosing a *Phurba*

Finding *phurbas* was once the exclusive privilege of those who traveled abroad. Thanks to our ever-shrinking world, they are now available through shops that provide dharma supplies to Buddhists, Himalayan craft stores, meditation suppliers, and various online vendors. You will want to choose this tool carefully. It is useful to look at a few before buying one, so it is best to shop around. You will want to decide on size, material (metal, wood, bone, crystal etc.), and the imagery represented on the *phurba*.

Once you have secured your *phurba*, journey to your teacher to get instructions for clearing and then empowering this spiritual implement. It is imperative to check what the spirits who will be supporting you in your use of the *phurba* want and to follow their directions carefully. When the ritual is done, tie cloth to the handle (usually red and white) to secure it for sacred purpose. Do another journey to ask how best to care for this tool, and then remember to make an offering to the spirits for their help and support.

Journey Explorations

- It is important to journey with your teacher or power animal to be introduced to the spirits that are represented on your *phurba*. Record what you learn from each of them.

- Under what circumstances does your spirit teacher want you to use the *phurba*?

Process Questions

- What drew you to the *phurba* have you chosen?

- What energies are represented on the pommel, handle, and blade?

Keep notes about how you work with the *phurba* and what changes and shifts you notice.

CHAPTER 15

The Long Staff and Wind Staffs

One element of a shaman's power regalia is a magical staff. Different forms are seen in cultures around the globe. From the deep jungles of the Amazon basin to the steppes of Asia, the deserts of Australia, and even to the high reaches of the Arctic, shamans use staffs as power objects. When the shaman's helping spirits work through these objects, it is possible to amplify the spiritual power that is available to the working shaman. As the shaman continues to use a staff in this manner, the object itself becomes inspirited. Since these objects are then considered to be alive, they function as assistants, partners, and guides to the shaman in her or his work and, as such, must be cared for as living beings.

For many peoples, the shaman's staff is a representation of the connection between the heavens and the Earth. Indeed, in many cultures, the spiritual realms are thought of as connected by a central axis or World Tree. This central column of the cosmos unites not only the realms of the Upper, Middle, and Lower Worlds of Spirit but also functions as the hub for the cardinal directions, the wheel of existence, and the still point around which the stars move. In essence it unites and holds the cosmos together. This central axis of the worlds, or *axis mundi*, provides a counterbalance to the forces of chaos that are simultaneously pulling the cosmos apart into its constituent components. It may be said that the World Tree gives form to life.

So a shaman's staff both represents and functions as the World Tree. As is the case with all true power objects, the staff is imbued with spiritual purpose and becomes a living presence. It becomes a catalyst for change and transformation—even capable of working on its own on behalf of the shaman.

In the Amazon, the shaman's staff, or *baculo*, is made from a six-foot length of wood that is ceremonially cut from *pona* or *chonta-kilo* wood, which many peoples in the region see as especially sacred. The staff is also decorated with special symbols, talismans, and carvings that signify the shaman's connections to power. For these people, the staff represents a connection to the Pleiades—a constellation that many Lower Amazonian people believe is their spiritual home according to the teachings of Don Agustin Rivas Vasquez. The staff functions as an energy conduit between the up above and down below worlds. As the stand-in for the *axis mundi*, World Tree, or center of the cosmos, it holds the spiritual center in ceremony.

Shamans from the First Nations of the Pacific Northwest of North America, such as the Tlingit and Haida, use staffs that are carved with representations of the shamans' spiritual connections along their length. These staffs allow the shaman to access ancestral spirits for help and guidance while performing shamanic healings. These staffs may be made of carved wood, whalebone, or ivory and are carried by the shaman during ceremonies. Ranging from fifteen inches to over forty inches, these implements are used to heal, combat the spirits of disease, and detect the presence of witchcraft or negative magic. Because of their role in combat, some of these objects are carved to resemble weapons such as clubs and long knives. Others are simple, long, and graceful arcs of bone or ivory completely covered in the carved images of the shaman's helping spirits and clan affiliation symbols.[40]

Figure 67. Enets iron shaman staff. (Pen and ink ©2013 Evelyn C. Rysdyk)

Among the Selkups, Enets, and Nenets of Siberia, the shaman's staff is her tree of life and functions as a support in the spirit journey while the shaman negotiates the perils of the trip to the spirit world of the ancestors. In the shamanic traditions of these people, the land between this world and the spiritual realms is harsh, with many sharp mountains and ravines separating the place of the dead from our world. Since the shamans in this region sing and dance their journeys, the staff also functions as a rhythm stick. To facilitate this role, the staff is forged of iron and covered in iron rings that clang together and against the body of the staff. Thus the staff takes the place of the shaman's drum while the journey is undertaken. These staffs are three to five feet tall, and some end in the form of a reindeer hoof at their base. As these peoples are reindeer herders, it represents a connection to the spirit of the animal on which each tribe relies.[41]

Among Grandfather Misha's people—the Ulchi of southeastern Siberia—the sacred objects are most often made from the wood of the most sacred tree in the taiga—the larch. While shamans' costumes are constructed of intricately sewn and embroidered cloth or fish skins, most of each shaman's other regalia—the drum hoop, rattles, extraction brooms made from shaved sticks, spirit figure carvings, and drum paddles—are all carved from larch wood. The shaman's staff is no exception.

During a healing, or *kamlanie* (Russian), the Ulchi shaman's shoulder-high staff is used as a place for the shaman's spirits to sit so that they may ride along while she or he travels into the forest or taiga. Like birds perched in a tree, they stand by the shaman—ever present and ready should the shaman need their help. Among the Ulchi the staff functions as a connector of the realms and also as a healing implement much like the way the drumbeater or drum itself is. Since the objects such as the staff are imbued with spiritual energy, they can work as partners with the shaman. In his healings, Grandfather Misha would use these objects to touch and brush a patient as a part of a healing.

The ancient Icelandic sagas tell us about the use of staffs in the shamanic rituals of the ancient Norse and Germanic peoples of Europe. Among these tribes, the ceremonial staff is the tool of the *völva*, or seeress. The *völva* is person who—while in a shamanic trance—enters the roots of the great World Tree Yggdrasil to gain access to ancestral wisdom. The ritual in which this prophecy is received is known as *seiðr* (pronounced "saythr"). This oracular ceremony was usually performed by specially gifted women—and very rarely by men—who, when in trance acted as the goddess Freyja, the Norse and Germanic goddess of the Earth who is both the giver and taker of life and the original shaman. Since she knows what the three Norns (Fates) will weave, she is also the goddess of prophecy and the patroness of the *völva*. The seer's costume includes a tall staff that is typically set with stones and bound in brass known as a *völ*, which is a critical part of the ritual since the ceremonial title *völva*, literally means "staff bearer."[42]

Contemporary Western spirit walkers may choose to use a staff or walking stick as a part of their shamanic paraphernalia. These can be either quite simply made of a length of wood from a tree that has significance to the shaman or may be elaborately decorated. They may have jingles that keep time to the shaman's dance or carry amulets to amplify the shaman's power. As with all other shamanic tools, they are as individually unique as the people who carry them.

Figure 68. A maple sapling, bittersweet, and reindeer antler staff. (Pen and ink © 2013 Evelyn C. Rysdyk)

One of my staffs is made from a maple sapling entwined by a bittersweet vine. This is significant to me as it reminds me of several themes. Bittersweet, *Celastrus orbiculatus*, is a showy, ornamental vine that was imported to the United States from Asia in 1860. Today, it is a prolific plant pest that slowly strangles native trees. For me, the vine-wrapped sapling reflects both the vulnerability we all have to the slow progress of age and disease as well as the ability that gentle forces have to overcome something large or seemingly impossible. It also reminds me that we are affected by those beings that accompany us on our life walk—that is, our environment shapes us as much as our genetics. The bittersweet vine also represents how poignant elements of our lives walk side by side with the many joys life has to offer.

On the top of my staff is a branch of reindeer antler. This is to honor my northern European roots as well as to provide a symbolic representation of the branches of the World Tree. The only other decoration is a bunch of silver bells that are attached to the staff with a loop of reindeer leather. These make a joyful sound whenever the staff is moved and so accompany my healing songs very nicely. When I am out walking in nature, however, I remove the bells so that I won't frighten animals and birds.

Whether you require the use of a staff to steady your steps or the World Tree is calling your heart into relationship, a staff may augment and enrich your spiritual life. Since it is capable of carrying power, it is important to choose your staff thoughtfully. If possible, I recommend that you create the staff yourself. There is tremendous power in crafting your own power objects. Sacred items you personally create hold an even deeper significance.

Exercise: Choosing a Shaman Staff

If your staff is meant to be of wood, go out onto land on which you have determined it is both safe and legal to harvest wood.

Prepare yourself by wearing the right outdoor clothing and sturdy walking shoes. Bring your rattle, your offering materials, a notebook, and food and water for yourself. If it is unfamiliar land, bring a map and compass or GPS receiver so that you won't get lost. It is also a good idea to let someone else know when you are going and where you'll be, just to be extra safe.

When you get to the land but prior to stepping onto it, make an offering to the spirits of place and let them know your intent. Reverently step onto the land and begin connecting with the tree spirits. Each species of tree has a different energy. Notice what varieties of trees draw you. For instance, are you pulled to the willows bending over the river, the sturdy oaks spreading their canopies over the forest, or the fir tree bristling with cones? When a specific tree has been chosen, ask that living being for permission to have some of its wood. Look around under the tree. A branch may be there ready for you to harvest. In any case, only cut the flesh of a tree when no other source is possible. Before you cut its flesh with knife or saw, make an offering and pray aloud your thanksgiving to the tree. As you are cutting, sing the tree your power song. This lets the spirit of the tree know who you are and the sacred heart-place from which you are working. As you are singing, cut the branch thoughtfully. Take this action with great care and reverence. Only take what you absolutely need and no more. When you are through, leave another heartfelt offering of gratitude, such as a small bit of food or drink behind to thank the tree for its sacrifice. I find that carrying a pocketful of birdseed is handy for such occasions.

If your staff is meant to be of another substance such as metal, use prayer or meditation to connect with the right one for you. One of my students made a remarkable staff from copper piping. At the top, she used a copper fitting as a seat for a large crystal, and at the bottom she placed a copper cap. Before all the soldering was completed, she filled the pipe with sacred stones and amulets. As it is moved over a patient, the objects in the staff shift and make a soft rain stick sound.

Once you have secured your staff, ask it how it might wish to be decorated. This can be done by drumming yourself into a journey state and asking your spirit teacher for advice. You may also ask your spirit teacher to take you to the spirit of your staff and ask it how it wants to be decorated. As you connect with the staff, you may find that you are asked to paint it, carve it, wrap it in beadwork, wood-burn symbols on it, tie bells on it, or hang objects such as feathers from its top. Follow the guidance you receive, and the staff will be just right for you.

Exercise: Empowering Your Staff

Once it has been decorated, it is time to empower your staff. Start as before with a gratitude offering to the spirits. Use your rattle or bell to honor all the helpful spirits that surround you and the tree who gave of its flesh as you sing your power song and merge with your power animal.

While you are singing, stand with your forehead touching one end of the staff and the other end on the floor. Journey back to the tree that carried the branch you now hold. Ask the tree to reveal its life force. Touch that life force and allow a small amount of it to enter your cupped hand. Close your hand around it, hold it to your heart, and return quickly to ordinary reality. Place your cupped hand on the top of the staff and blow the tree's life force energy into the staff. Use your inner eye to see a ball of light energy flowing into the stick. When you are done, rattle around the staff with the intention of sealing the energy in.

Now hold your staff vertically, and honor the vital the energies and helping spirits of the Upper, Middle, and Lower Worlds as they connect through the center of your staff. Start singing your power song again and tap the staff on the ground/floor to the beat of the song. You and your staff are at the center of your shamanic universe. Feel the power whirling all around you and empowering the staff. Invite your spirit teacher and power animal to join you. Ask them to connect their energies to the staff. When the process is complete, beat the rhythm of the callback, unmerge, and return yourself to ordinary reality.

Upon your return at the callback signal, take ample time to sit with the experience. Do this before you attempt to write anything down in your notebook. Make an offering of gratitude outside and thank all the spirits for their participation with you. Let your heart fill with gratitude for the gifts you have received.

As soon as you can, spend some quiet time alone in nature with this new part of your life. Allow yourself to reexperience the connections between the shamanic realms or spirit and the flow of those energies. Notice what happens inside your body. Be patient, and over time you will more deeply sense the strength of the great World Tree in your hand. Allow this new part of your life to become a reminder of your personal connections to All That Is.

Journey Explorations

- Journey to a teacher or power animal to ask: "What are the ways I am to use this staff in my shamanic practice?" Record the content of your journey and your perceptions about what you receive.

- Journey to a teacher or power animal to ask: "What is the best way to care for my staff's spirit?" Make notes on what you receive.

- Journey to a teacher or power animal to ask: "How is my staff connected to the World Tree?"

After each journey, go out on the land with your staff to make an offering to the spirits.

Staffs for the Four Winds

When a shaman is called to work with natural forces, using a staff or wand is an excellent way to modify the raw power enough for it to be more safely utilized. When accessing the powers of the elementals, I often am guided to use the staffs from my *mesa*. I hold them while I journey and apply them as directed by my teaching spirits. For instance, I was asked to bring one of my staffs connected to the water elemental outside to help encourage rain during a drought.

Those of you who have read and done the exercises in my previous book *Spirit Walking: A Course in Shamanic Power* have met the spirits of the Four Winds and can proceed to the directions for making staffs. If you haven't had the opportunity to meet the winds, do the following journeys to the North, East, South, and West winds.

Journey to a teacher or power animal and ask it to take you to meet with the spirit of the each of the winds. Don't try to do these all in one day! Each wind carries the energy of one of the elementals more strongly and will be best suited to support your work with that elemental. Take time to meet and get acquainted with each wind and in so doing begin to get acquainted with the elemental forces.

Have your teacher or power animal introduce you. Once you have been introduced to the spirit of the each wind, ask the spirit the following questions.

"How may I work with you safely?"

"How do I honor you?"

"How can you help me?"

"How may we work together in harmony?"

After you have gotten your answers, thank the spirit of the wind you met and return to ordinary reality. After you have made notes and grounded yourself, go out and do an offering of gratitude. Follow up with anything that you received from the spirit of the wind.

Exercise: Making Wind Staffs

Since you have met the Four Winds, it is time to create staffs that represent the individual winds as well as all that you know about each direction. I recommend that you collect wood for your staffs from trees that have powerful connections to the direction of each wind or to your journeys with each of the winds. For instance, based upon my experience an evergreen is an excellent choice for the North, as is the root of a large tree or one that has grown through a rock.

As you prepare to create each staff, gather the wood with intention, as you gathered your shaman walking staff. Always harvest fallen wood whenever you can, since you do not want to disturb the forest. Only cut the flesh of a tree when no other source is possible. Remember to be respectful and do honoring rituals to the spirits of the forest and the individual tree with gratitude for their gift to you.

Once you have a stick in hand that will be the basis for your first staff, journey to a teacher or power animal to ask, "How do I make a staff to honor the _____ Wind?"

Awakening the Stick

After you have returned and done your offering, begin gathering the materials you will need. As you did with the wood itself, remember to treat all of the materials with respect. Once all the materials are in hand, set aside time to work on your staff in a good way. Honor the spirits, prepare your space and yourself for sacred work, and then awaken the stick. This ritual for enlivening is a method that was taught to us by a student of the shamanic rabbi Gershon Winkler.

Materials and Tools

- Shamanic journey recording

- Blindfold

- Your stick

- Your rattle

- Notebook and writing implement

Empower the Staff

Sit on the floor with your blindfold on, the journey recording ready, your stick in your hand, and your rattle nearby. Position yourself so that one end of the stick is on the floor while the other end is touching your forehead. Start the recording.

Begin a journey by connecting with your power animal or teacher and asking to be taken to the spirit of the tree that once held this stick. Travel into the tree and down to its roots. When you are in the roots, gather some of the light that is held there into your free hand. Immediately return to ordinary reality and blow the light into the end of the stick that was against your forehead.

Rattle around the stick to seal in the light and then rattle the callback to help bring you back to ordinary reality. Make notes of what you have experienced, and then honor the spirit of the tree with an offering in nature.

Now that the stick is fully alive, you can actually start creating the staff following the instructions given to you by your teacher. Take time to be in gratitude and then ask your teacher or power animal to assist you in empowering and decorating your staff as you have done with your other sacred tools. Once the staff is empowered, take journeys to find answers to the following questions.

- "How do I work with this staff safely?"

- "When is the right time to use this staff?"

Following the method you used with the first wind, meet with each spirit of the Four Winds as you are ready to make their staffs. In each case follow these steps to enliven the stick and then proceed with the instructions of your teachers and power animals in how to decorate and empower it.

Using Your Staffs

Once you have completed all four staffs, you will have a new and powerful set of shamanic tools. These four direction staffs that you have created may be used for many purposes. Placed in a room at each of the four directions, the staffs can dedicate the area as sacred space. Such a spiritually dedicated space can be used to calm, support healing, make a space more conducive to prayer and meditation, or provide extra power for your creative projects. The staffs can also be used outdoors to delineate an area for ritual work.

Staffs like yours may be used to heal you when guided by the spirits of your power animals and teachers. In addition, they may be called upon in difficult times to draw more power to yourself so that you are more able to hold your center and stay grounded.

As with all other shamanic tools, it is imperative to work with these in conjunction with your helper spirits. As a shamanic practitioner, your work is always carried out with the guidance and support of these beings. When we work in concert with them, we create a team that is the best of the visible and invisible realms. When we join our physicality with the spirits' perspective, we are kept safe and are far less likely to cause inadvertent harm to ourselves or any other being. Indeed, while we can harm others, no person—not a doctor or shaman—can really heal another being. All we can ever do is to provide the best possible conditions and supports so that the patient's inner healer is able to regenerate the body and mind. I cannot stress this enough. While this truth is humbling, it is imperative to hold in the forefront of your consciousness.

My friend and teacher Bhola Banstola speaks about shamanic healing in this way:

> *The shaman, in his altered state of consciousness, travels*
> *through landscapes, symbols, colors, shadows and lights.*
> *During this journey they try to find the cause of the cli-*
> *ent's problems and through songs, metaphors, and sym-*
> *bolic actions they bring balance and harmony to their*
> *clients. . . . Shamans are not really the healers; they are*
> *the facilitators and creators of the sacred space within*
> *which an individual can receive the healing energies*
> *brought by the spirits. Healing is not only meant for cur-*
> *ing the affected body parts, but also should bring about*
> *a profound harmony between the spiritual, emotional,*
> *energetic and soul parts.*

If you find that a circumstance is calling you to use the
staffs for supporting a healing in yourself, listen to your heart
to make sure that this step is truly right and timely in your
process.

Exercise: Using the Staffs for Healing Yourself

Journey to your teacher and/or power animal to ask: "How may
I use my staffs to help facilitate healing me?"

When you return from your journey, take the time to write
down what you have received and do an offering of gratitude.
Then, sit for a while with your staffs in your lap to get connected to them as healing tools. In order to follow through
with the instructions you received from your spirits, there are
steps that you have to follow to do *any* shamanic healing work.
These preparatory steps will support the work in being clear,
safe, and powerful.

Perform a Shamanic Healing for Yourself with Your Staffs

1. Gather your staffs and other shamanic paraphernalia.

2. Journey before you work to get your teacher's instructions.

3. Prepare the space in which you will be working by honoring the spirits of the directions with your rattle. You may also wish to light a candle. The lighting of a flame helps us to remember that we are first and foremost beings of light who are a part of a fabric of light that encompasses All That Is.

4. Sing and dance with your spirits to enliven your energy and to bring yourself fully into the experience.

5. Once you feel prepared, follow through with the healing instructions that you received from your helper spirits.

6. Take time to check in with yourself after the healing. You may want to have a glass of water and rest after the healing to allow the work that was done by the spirits and your staffs to assimilate into your being. Notice how you feel.

7. Make an offering of gratitude.

8. Continue to notice your feelings and thoughts for a few days and record them in your journal along with any insights that you have received.

Process Questions

- Articulate, as best as you can, in your journal, the bodily, emotional, and spiritual sensations of receiving a healing by the winds through your staffs.

- How has this healing shifted your perceptions about the winds?

- How has this healing shifted your perceptions about your sacred objects? Record what you have noticed.

CHAPTER 16

Shamans' Costumes

A shaman's costume is perhaps the most individually unique element of the shaman's paraphernalia. While many contemporary practitioners wear ordinary street clothes when they do their work, usually some form of ritual garb is worn while performing a shamanic healing. This act of donning a special article of clothing—or a complete costume, on occasion—alters one's visual appearance, and is a physical reminder or reflection of the fact that the shaman becomes *another*—that is, the shaman has become the embodiment of the healing spirits with which she or he works. This alteration of physical appearance has parallels in the clothing worn by Christian clerics when they perform sacred rites. When a priest kisses and places the mantle or stole of his office over his head, he signals with this action both his connection to and ability to interpret for the Divine. He becomes *holy*—he takes on the *mantle of spirit*—by the same action that shamans have used for many millennia.

Some of the most elaborate examples of the shaman's costumes are found among the tribes of Siberia. In her 1914 work *Aboriginal Siberia, A Study in Social Anthropology*, the young anthropologist M.A. Czaplicka offered descriptions of costumes from several of these tribal groups. It is important to note that there is a belief among the people of Asia that the first shaman was a woman. This is reflected in the costume of the shaman as well as the language that is sometimes used to refer to a male shaman. A male Chukchee shaman, for instance, is called *yirka-laul-vairgin*, which roughly translates to "soft man."[43] This reflects that the duties of the shaman require taking on what we in the West might call feminine energy and what people of that region saw as the need for changing sex. A female shaman's connection to the spirits was seen as so strong that in some cases—among the Chukchee and Koriak, for instance—women shaman did not even require costumes. Referring to this connection between femaleness and shamanism, Czaplicka shares what the earlier Russian ethnographer Troshchanski found among the Yakut (Sakha) people: "On the shaman's apron there are sewn two iron circles representing breasts" and "the man-shaman dresses his hair like a woman, on the two sides of his head and braids it; during a performance he lets the hair fall down."[44] Across Asia, the costumes of many shamans resemble a woman's dress, often with aprons and long skirts as a primary element.

Among the Mongol people, the shaman wears a skirt of long strips of cloth. Each of the strips is pointed at the hem to resemble a very long silk necktie. These skirts twirl, flap, and rise as the shaman dances.[45] Like the long tassels, ribbons, and fringe on a Siberian costume, they help the shaman to "fly" into the realm of the spirits. In addition, they may help witnesses to the shaman's work visually relate him or her to the great birds of prey that are symbols of power.

A Yakut shaman's coat, as described by Czaplicka, is made from leather. It is shorter in the front, just reaching the knees, and longer in the back, reaching all the way to the ground. Although simple in overall shape, it is quite elaborately decorated, being covered in many forged iron amulets and ornaments. Between

Figure 69. This metal figure of a spirit guardian of the shamanic river that separated the worlds of the living and dead is from an Evenk shaman's costume. It is engraved to indicate the dismembered spirit body of those that walk between the realms—the spirit walkers themselves. (From a photo from the 1997 exhibition *Journey to Other Worlds*, Illinois State Museum, in conjunction with the Russian Museum of Ethnography. Pen and ink ©2013 Evelyn C. Rysdyk)

the shoulders, the shaman wore an image of the sun as a round, shiny disk hung on a leather strap, threaded through a hole in the center of the disk. Beneath this was hung another disk of the same size referred to as the Hole-in-the-ice Sun with a larger central hole and longer strap. Across the back, above the waist, hung rolls of iron as thick as a thumb but longer and long, thin iron plates. Just below the collar were suspended copper bells without clappers. They are as large as crow eggs and have engravings of fish heads at the top. These are also tied onto the costume with leather. Two small flat disks are sewn to the shoulders like epaulets. On each side of the shaman's costume are sewn iron plates that are about three inches square. The sleeves are ornamented in a similar fashion with longer plates. Since the example comes from a *kenniki oyuun*, or most powerful kind of shaman, it also had a *ämügyat*, or amulet, sewn to the breast of the costume as a representation of the shaman's most powerful protector spirit. In fact the same word is used to refer both to the amulet and to the spirit itself. This amulet is a plate of copper that is engraved with the image of this human-form spirit. This spirit from the Upper World is the one the shaman calls upon for healing. It is only when the shaman is intentionally possessed by this spirit that he begins his frenzied dancing.

The back of the costume also has a yard-long iron plate forged in the shape of a fish hung vertically so that it drags on the ground. This dragging fish works like a lure, helping to entice the shaman's other helping spirits into this realm. The back of the coat is finished in long fringes that extend to the ground. These fringes sometimes end in copper balls. The remaining areas of the costume are covered in cloth and leather appliqués of animals, birds, fishes, stars, moons, and suns. There are also representations of the human skeleton and viscera that have been forged in iron as well. These represent the psycho-spiritual dismemberment the shaman experiences in his initiation.[46]

Adding to the overall noise produced by the iron elements sewn onto the costume, the iron bustles worn by shamans across Siberia, Tuva, Mongolia, and China are seen as essential elements of a shaman's costume. When the shaman shakes her or his hips during an ecstatic, trance-induced, and trance-sustaining dance, these heavy bustles jangle loudly. These remarkable articles of the shaman's costume are made from a leather belt with a large flap in the back. Over this flap is hung a large cluster of metal objects. Known in the Ulchi language as a *yampa* or *yompa*, this bustle provides a constant accompaniment to the drumming, dancing, and singing of the shaman.

Grandfather Misha's *yompa* belt had dozens of iron cones as long as my hand that rang against each other and an ancient bronze shaman's mirror from China that was the size of a luncheon plate. The accumulation of all this iron and bronze made Grandfather Misha's *yompa* quite heavy for his diminutive frame. Those that wear these forms of ritual apparel have to be quite strong, and this physical strength is tied to the shaman's overall ability to perform well. It is said that in order to be a good shaman, one's costume had to contain thirty-five to forty pounds of iron. In fact, there is an old Sakha (Yakut) proverb that says, "Blacksmiths and shamans are of the same nest."[47] However, the blacksmith first gained his power by creating the ornaments for a female shaman's costume. His contact with ritual objects gave him some shamanic power of his own.[48]

The Ulchi *yompa* is composed of many different pieces, each of which has its own name. These include eight- to ten-inch-long pieces of iron that have been rolled into cone-like forms, iron rods, actual bells, and in some cases ancient Chinese bronze discs with auspicious symbols cast on their faces. The iron cones which often dominate the bustle are called *kongoro*, the rods are called *kyrie*, the links are *tasso*, circular disks are referred to as *tole*, and copper bells are called *kongokto*.[49]

In addition to its use as an accompaniment to the shamanic trance, the bustle may clear the shaman of intrusive energy. This is usually done at the close of a healing. In many cultures, the shaman engages in combat against the spirits of illness while performing the healing. In this combat, when they are wrestling with the evil spirits of disease, shamans believe that they are at risk, and so they depend upon the strength of their helping spirits to keep them safe. In order for the connection to these harmful spirits to be assuredly broken—so that they are not brought back by the returning shaman to this realm—the shaman performs some form of cleansing or "saving" of himself as a part of the closing ritual. The Ulchi shaman Grandmother Tikka would beat her back with the *yompa* to drive out any illness that might be clinging to her, and Manchu shamans toss the iron-filled bustle over their back to their assistants at the close of a healing.[50] This behavior has the effect of confounding the spirits that might be clinging to it, thus chasing them away as well.

The Nganasan shaman's coat resembles that of the Yakut in many ways. It is decorated with many amulets of iron and bone and also bears a length of iron chain fastened to the back. This chain is either held by the shaman's human helpers or tied to a rafter in the building during the shaman's trance. This chain anchors the shaman to this realm for the return trip after his battle with the spirits of disease. An Altaian shaman's costume is made of reindeer hide. Like the Yakut coat, it is covered in many amulets, some of which are small doll-like figures of the sha-man's spirit helpers. These are said to awaken when the jingles on the costume begin to sound during the shaman's dance.[51] The ethnographers Agapitoff and Khangaloff described an old Buryat shaman's costume of a kind that is no longer found. This particular coat was made of white cloth. The front was com-pletely covered in metal figures of horses, fishes, birds, and so on. The back was decorated with twisted iron strips—which were meant to represent snakes and several different kinds of bells. The chest of the costume had plates like ribs made of iron, and there were iron "bones" sewn to the arms.

The shamans of Pacific North America (the Tlingit, Tsimshian, Kwakiutl, Nootka, Haida, and other tribes) wear aprons, which echo the Siberian shamans' apron and coat. These aprons, put on like skirts around the waist, are made of hide that is most often painted with the images of spirits and sometimes decorated in dentaliums. Over the top of this are tied numerous amulets and figures of the spirits that have been carved from bone. These click together when the shaman dances in much the same manner as the Siberian shaman's iron decorations. These aprons end in very long fringe. Each of these fringes may also terminate in a puffin beak decoration. These hornlike beaks clatter together during the shaman's work and function like additional rattles.[52] Over the top of this apron, the shamans of this region sometimes wore poncho-like tunics of painted hide or woven cedar bark capes or a large animal fur wrapped around the body.

Figure 70. Evenk shaman's cap. (Pen and ink ©2013 Evelyn C. Rysdyk)

Some shamans wear headdresses or caps as a part of their ritual garb. In the north of Siberia, the shaman wears a cap like the woman's traveling cap, or *tusakta*[53] as it is called among the Yakut (Sakha) people. This cap has earflaps and may also have long fringe that hangs in front of the face. This fringe, which may be made of leather, cloth, or fur strips, helps the shaman to stay removed from ordinary reality and resembles a woman's bangs. This is to honor the magic woman shaman who is believed to be the original, primordial shaman in many Eurasian shamanic traditions. The cap of the Altaian shaman is a square piece of hide from a reindeer calf. On one side are buttons, and the other, loops. When fastened with the buttons in the back, the hat becomes cylinder-shaped. This hat is decorated with bunches of feathers which stand erect once the hat is buttoned and a fringe mask of string and shells which hangs from the bottom. Among the Teleut, the cap is made of a brown owl's skin with the head still intact. This particular headgear is only worn by the highest and most powerful of Teleut shamans.[54] Since the shaman often works during the night hours and takes flight during trance, the owl would be seen as especially well suited to the shaman's work.

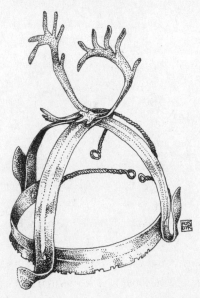

Figure 71. Siberian shaman's crown. (Pen and ink ©2013 Evelyn C. Rysdyk)

Some Siberian shamans and those of the more southerly tribes such as the Buryat, Mongol, and Manchu people, wear metal, fur, and cloth crowns. Once constructed in heavy iron, these are now usually made of lighter weight, thinner metals like copper and brass. These crowns are fashioned as a band around the brow and two interlocking, crossed bands of the same metal over the top of the head. The tops may terminate in antlers, like the Siberian caps described earlier, or in tree, bird, or other nature motifs. Among the Buryat, Mongol, and Manchu, these crowns are further decorated with long streamers of colorful silk that hang down the back and shoulders of the shamans. Like the ribbons and fringes of the costume, these streamers swirl around as the shaman dances.

The tribal people of the North American Pacific coast also wear crowns as a part of their traditional shaman's costume. This shamanic headgear is usually composed of a circlet of tines sewn onto a leather band. These tines—which can be grizzly bear claws or bone, antler, horn, abalone shell rim, or ivory representations of claws—face upward toward the sky. Like other crowns, this reflects the intention to connect with the spirits of "heaven" or the Upper World of spirit. As with other parts of a shaman's ritual garb, these crowns are also invested with curing powers.[55]

In 1914, Czaplicka, wrote, "In everyday life the shaman is not distinguishable from other people . . . but when he is engaged in communicating with spirits he has to make use of a special dress and special instruments."[56] Later on in the text she enumerates the following items as "indispensable to the shaman's dress all over Siberia—the coat, the mask, the cap, and the copper or iron plate on the breast. The Samoyed (Selkup) . . . substitute for the mask a handkerchief tied over the eyes, so that they can penetrate into the spirit-world by their inner sight."

Czaplicka writes later on in the same chapter,

The whole costume with its appurtenances (accessories) used during shamanistic performances throughout Siberia has, according to Mikhailowski,[57] a threefold significance:

- *The shaman wishes to make a profound impression on the eyes of the people by the "eccentricity" of his costume.*

- *The ringing of the bells and the noise of the drum impress their sense of hearing.*

- *Finally, a symbolic meaning is attached to these accessories and adornments, a meaning known only to believers, especially to the shamans, and closely connected with the religious conceptions of shamanism.*

She addresses the simplified and somewhat condescending approach of Mikhailowski by further adding:

> *But this interpretation does not bring out the whole importance of the relation of these objects to the spiritual world. They are of great importance, for the spirits will not bear the voice of the shaman unless the right dress and implements are used, and the drum beaten; they are sacred because of their contact with a supernatural and often dangerous power.*

> *Being sacred, the [shaman's] accessories must not be used by anyone but a shaman otherwise they are impotent to produce any result. It is only a good shaman, a real one, who can possess the full shaman's dress.*

Exercise: Creating Ritual Clothing

I believe that the ritual clothing of a shaman is a direct outgrowth of her or his relationship with the spirits and their power. Furthermore, the shaman's paraphernalia increases the power available as the clothing, implements, and instruments, such as the drum, have been enlivened. This empowerment invests the objects with the essential energies of the shaman's helping spirits.

As you grow in your practice, you will eventually require some form of shamanic clothing to augment your connections to power. This can be a vest, shirt, overcoat, dress, apron, or some other form of clothing that has been created and decorated in a sacred way and empowered. The best way to find out what will work for you and the spirits with whom you work is to journey to them to ask questions. Here are some suggested journeys:

- Journey to a teacher or power animal to ask: "What shamanic ritual clothing is right for me?"

- Journey to a teacher or power animal to ask: "At what times am I to use my ritual clothing?"

- Journey to a teacher or power animal to ask: "How do I make (or find) my ritual clothing?"

- Journey to a teacher or power animal to ask: "How is this ritual clothing to be decorated?"

- Journey to a teacher or power animal to ask: "How do I care for this ritual clothing?"

Figure 72. Ai Churek's costume was decorated with dozens of long cloth cords sewn to the bottoms of the sleeves, along the back, and to either side of the front of her coat. The cords moved when she danced and drummed and echoed her movements. (Pen and ink ©2013 Evelyn C. Rysdyk)

Record the content of each journey and your perceptions about what you receive.

On the day you set aside for making and/or decorating your ritual clothing, create sacred space before you begin. Assemble the materials and tools that you will need while remaining in a prayerful attitude. If you are starting with an existing piece of clothing, ritually cleanse the garment by merging with your teacher and asking for it to be cleared of anything that is not useful to your sacred purpose.

Make an offering before you begin preparing the clothing. Proceed with creating and decorating and make another offering when you have completed the article of clothing.

Exercise: Empowering Your Ritual Clothing

At this point, your new regalia should be enlivened and empowered for its sacred purpose.

1. When you are ready to dedicate your new article of ritual clothing, make a gratitude offering to the spirits. Call with your heart to bring your power animal to you. Give thanks to him or her and to the natural world for your connections with spiritual power.

2. Put on the garment and begin a journey to your spirit teacher. Shake your rattle or bell or play your drum to accompany your journey. Dance and sing to thank this spirit who has chosen to meet with you!

3. Once you are with your spirit teacher, ask to merge to empower the clothing. Allow the teacher to bless it for sacred work.

4. When the process feels complete, thank the spirits and begin shaking your rattle or bell or drumming to the

rhythm of the journey callback signal. Fully unmerge from your spirit teacher and return yourself to ordinary reality.

Upon your return, take ample time to sit with the experience prior to recording it in your notebook. Remember to go outside and make an offering of thanks. Let your heart fill with gratitude for the gifts you have received in this experience and place an offering on the Earth with reverence.

Process Questions

- What did it feel like to empower your ritual clothing?

- How do you feel when you wear this clothing now that it is empowered? How has it changed your relationship to your teacher and power animal?

- How are you meant to care for this clothing? Are their special circumstances in your spirit walking practice that will be enhanced by wearing this garment?

As you continue to work with your ritual clothing and your other implements, keep a journal of what you realize about your own process. This is important, as self-knowledge is one of the keys to being a powerful spirit walker. Remember to remain humble about your shamanic gifts, as a truly powerful person has no need to show off. The relationships that you cultivate with the spirits are strengthened by humility, compassion, and through diligent practice of all you are learning in the pages of this book.

Conclusion

"In every age and clime, among every race, there have been those who have sought to know more of the truths around, above and in them—[people] who have risen above their fellows, and have been looked up to as leaders and advisors of the rest. We need not wonder then that Shamanism [is] so prevalent."[58]

—JAMES CHESTON MORRIS, SPEAKING IN 1897

Thanks to widespread industrialization and the destruction of wild areas across our planet, it is no accident that beginning in the latter part of the 20th century, we have seen a growing resurgence in shamanism. People around the world are being draw to explore the spiritual ties that bind us to our environment. We are learning the ways of our ancestors; conversing with the spirits of the plants, animals, and birds; and listening to the voices of the wind and water. The more we reach out to "all our relations," the more deeply humbled we are by the splendor that Mother Earth provides us.

Now more than ever, we need people like you who are willing to listen to the spirits and, through living their lives in harmony, model for the larger culture a path toward one of balance and peace. May many wonderful blessings flow to and through you as you beat your drum, dance, shake your rattle, sing your songs, make your offerings, and pray your gratitude for all creation.

BLESSINGS TO YOU ON YOUR JOURNEYS,
EVELYN C. RYSDYK

Tribal shamans mentioned in this book

Aama Bombo (1939–). Born Buddhi Maya Lama, Aama Bombo (Mother Shaman) is a woman of Tibetan ancestry born in Melung, Nepal. She is a member of the International Council of 13 Indigenous Grandmothers. Her father was a renowned Tamang shaman, and she works with the same spirits who once worked with him to do her healing. In spite of the prohibition that Tamang culture has against female shamans, Aama Bombo felt the spirits enter her body when she was twenty-five years old. As healer who still sees as many as one hundred clients in a day in her home, she says of her work with the wider world: "I am doing my prayers around the world to create a world without war and tension. I want to see this world full with natural beauty, where everybody will have equal rights and opportunity to share nature's womb." I was fortunate to meet and receive a healing from her while in Nepal in 2012.

Ai Churek (1963–2011). Ai Churek (Moon Heart) was one of the most powerful shamans from Tuva. She founded the Tos Deer (Nine Heavens) Shamanic Center in her country's capital of Kyzyl. Daughter of a traditional shaman woman, Ai Churek was born in the taiga of southern Siberia and from an early age exhibited her mother's gift for communicating with spirits and the animal world, at a time when the Soviet Union maintained a rigidly atheistic dogma. Her mother died when she was a child, and relatives who did not understand her gift and instead tried to have her cured brought her up. Locked up in a psychiatric hospital, accused of being a witch, Ai Churek was finally banished to Moscow. After perestroika, she returned to Tuva in the 1990s, where Mongush B. Kenin-Lopsan, curator of the Museum of Shamanism of Tuva, finally recognized her gift. In 2004, I invited her to teach my students in Maine.

Bhola Nath Banstola (1966–). Bhola Nath Banstola is a Nepalese *jhankri* born in the Bhojpur district of east Nepal. He was called by the spirits at a very young age to become a shaman and was initiated by his grandfather, who was the shaman of the village. Educated in Nepal and India, Bhola holds a master's degree in cultural anthropology from the University of Delhi. He is also a graduate in naturopathy from the Indian Board of Alternative Medicines in Calcutta. Bhola travels extensively to teach the wisdom of his ancestors to groups in Europe and North America. I have been studying with him since 2007 in the United States and Nepal and have been hosting him to teach in Maine since 2008.

Eduardo Calderón Palomino (1930–1996). Don Eduardo was a fisherman, potter, and coastal shaman from Trujillo, Peru. He is best known for his elaborate San Pedro healing *mesa* ceremonies. Calderón and his work and life are discussed in depth in Douglas Sharon's book *Wizard of the Four Winds*. My initial study of Peruvian shamanism and the *mesa* ceremony (1991–94) was guided by one of his students, Don Roy Bauer of the Circle of the Sacred Earth. I was the assistant *curandera* in these ceremonies.

Fredy "Puma" Quispe Singona (1980–). Fredy "Puma" Quispe Singona is a Quechua-speaking Chavin Indian *paqo* (shaman/medicine man) born in the highlands of Chinchero, in the Andean region of Peru. From the age of six, he trained with his late grandfather, Maximo Quispe, in traditional Andean shamanic ways. He is a speaker and gives workshops about ancestral Inca healing and ways of global healing around the world. I sponsored him to teach in Maine in 2002.

Nyima Dhondup (1941–2013). "Pau" Nyima, a Tibetan *lhapa* (shaman/healer), was born in the Bungpa, Kepyang region of upper Tibet. He practiced a shamanic tradition that was passed down to him through his maternal bloodline. According to the blog maintained by his daughter, Tenzin Lhamo, he began to feel the spirits enter his body at age thirteen, and by age twenty-five the lama Sakya Trizin Gongma Rinpoche had formally recognized him as a shaman with the power of the mountain and hail deity Thang-lha-yab-shur (Thang Lha). He merged with this deity and several other spirits when he performed healings. I was fortunate to visit him at his home in the Tarshi Palkhiel Tibetan refugee settlement near Pokhara, Nepal in 2012 and was able to receive a healing from him.

Mikhail "Misha" Duvan (1901–1996). "Grandfather Misha" was the last male shaman of the Ulchi people of southeastern Siberia. He lived north of the city of Khabarovsk along the banks of the Amur River in Bulava village. Grandfather Misha did not become a shaman until he was in his thirties. Misha's parents died when he was a young boy, so he and his brother walked for days to the home of his grandfather who took them in. Misha's grandfather was a powerful thunder shaman who could call and control the rain and the thunder. Since his grandfather trained Grandfather Misha, he practiced indigenous traditions that predated the anti-shamanic Soviet era.

In spite of his advanced age and limited eyesight, Grandfather Misha could become powerfully inspirited to perform rituals or healings once he began drumming and singing his journey to the spirit world. I was very blessed to have studied with him in 1995. His reverence for nature and his deep humbleness still touch me deeply.

APPENDIX B

Glossary of terms

algysh. A Tuvan shamanic prayer song.

ämügyat. An amulet representing a Yakut shaman's spirit helper, which was typically sewn onto the shaman's costume. *Ämügyat* is also the name that is used for the spirit helper.

Aurignacian. A term used to describe an Upper Paleolithic human culture that existed in Europe and southwestern Asia 45,000-35,000 years ago.

axis mundi. A central unifying principle of the world's center and/or the connection between the heavens, the Earth, and lower realms. It is sometimes represented as a great tree. (*See also* World Tree.)

baculo. Amazonian shaman staff made from *Geonoma weberbaueri*, known in Spanish as *chonta-duro*.

Bon. A polytheistic Himalayan religion.

budtode. An Enets language term for an especially esteemed shaman.

callback signal. A final rhythm in shamanic journey drumming that supports the journeyer to return to ordinary consciousness.

cauyaq. An Alutiiq (Pacific coast Yup'ik) drum with a short handle.

chalama. A cloth braid used to dedicate a shaman tree in the central Asian region of Tuva and also the name for smaller offering braids that are tied to the tree.

chonta-kilo. Very durable, dense wood from the Amazonian *Geonoma weberbaueri* tree used for shaman staffs. This dense wood is very resistant to rot and so equated with the "Tree of Life."

chupshed or *chopshee.* The Nepalese term for the counter beads used on a *mala* or prayer bead strand to keep track of the number of chanted prayers or mantras.

curandera. A female Central or South American shamanic healer of the *curanderisimo* tradition who may also use herbal medicine.

curanderismo. A Central or South American shamanic healing tradition that may also include the use herbal medicine and hands-on healing.

curandero. A male Central or South American shamanic healer of the *curanderisimo* tradition who may also use herbal medicine.

despacho. A ritual offering bundle commonly used in Peru, Bolivia, and Ecuador.

dhyangro. A Nepalese shaman drum that has a *phurba* as a handle.

dorje. A Himalayan ritual object that symbolizes both the proprieties of a diamond, which is a representation of the idea of indestructibility, and a thunderbolt, which represents irresistible force. (*See also* vajra.)

Dorje Phurba. Also known as Vajrakilaya, this being is a wrathful deity who embodies the enlightened activity of all the Buddhas. This deity is able to remove obstacles, destroy the forces hostile to compassion, and purify spiritual pollution.

effigy. A figurative representation of a spirit or living entity.

empower. The action of imbuing an object with the spiritual essence of a protective or healing entity.

ezed. The Tuvan word for a spirit or a shamanic object containing a spirit. Spirits of the Earth that enliven a place are referred to as *Cher Ehzed.*

gau. A Himalayan spiritual object that can be worn, which holds prayers, small talismans, and deity images.

geespu. The flat, fur-covered drumbeater of an Ulchi shaman.

gievre. A Sami frame drum that has a frame made from a bent slab of green wood.

gimsacha. A larch-shaving wand used by Ulchi shamans to cleanse a patient during a healing.

goavdi. The unique bowl-shaped drum of the northern Sami people.

guovza. The Sami word for bear.

heargi. The Sami word for reindeer.

huaco silbador. A Peruvian whistling vessel used for expanding awareness.

jhankri. The Nepalese term for a shamanic healer.

kachina. Spirits of nature and natural phenomena honored by the Pueblo peoples of the American Southwest. Figures of these spirits are also called kachinas or kachina dolls.

kamlanie. The Russian word used to describe a shamanic healing ceremony.

kannu. A heavy Sami drum that has a frame made from a notched board.

kenniki oyuun. The most powerful kind of Yakut shaman.

kilaya. A ceremonial dagger with a triangular blade used in Himalayan shamanism and Buddhist and Bon rituals. It is also known as a *phurba*.

kongokto/kongoro. Rolled metal bells without clappers that are attached to a Siberian shaman's bustle. Specifically, *kongokto* are made from copper and *kongoro* are iron.

kyrie. Iron rods that accompany the metal bells on a Siberian shaman's bustle.

lávvu. The conical tent used by traditional, nomadic Sami reindeer herders.

lhapa. A Tibetan shaman. Nyima Dhondup was the last remaining *lhapa*. He lived as a Tibetan exile in Nepal.

lokur chuni. A special Himalayan medallion that has auspicious zodiac symbols on one side and a smooth mirrored finish on the reverse, typically used for personal protection.

mala. A Buddhist or Himalayan shamanic rosary.

melong. A Himalayan shaman mirror made of brass or silver. Typically used for protection, they may be any size from approximately two inches to over ten inches in diameter. The smooth side of a *lokur chuni* (see above) may be used for the same purpose.

mesa. The ritual and healing altar of a South American shaman that may contain as many as one hundred objects and implements.

noaidi. The Sami term for shaman.

ogham. An early medieval Celtic magical alphabet in which each letter correlates to a different species of tree.

ongon. A Siberian spirit effigy. These are thought to be the actual house for the spirit that they represent.

oova. A Tuvan term for a sacred cairn, large stone, or post erected on the landscape that is then used as a receptacle for offerings.

oovo. A Mongolian term for a sacred cairn, large stone, or post erected on the landscape which is then used as a receptacle for offerings.

Pachamama. A Quechua Indian term for Mother Earth.

paqo. The Quechua Indian term for a shaman from the Andes of South America.

Phi Faa. The feminine sky deity of Thailand and Laos.

phurba. A ceremonial dagger with a triangular blade used in Himalayan shamanism and Buddhist and Bon rituals. Also known as a *kilaya*.

power animal. A protective spirit of a shaman or spirit walker that may be accessed for guidance or merged with for personal protection or to "borrow" the animal's senses for the purpose of healing or divination.

qilaat. The Greenland Inuit word for the shaman's drum.

Quechua. The name of a people of the central Andes of South America and their languages.

quena. An end-blown flute commonly played in modern-day Peru.

rawhide. The scraped and dried hide of an animal. It is typically used for drumheads and may be found through companies that supply drum-making supplies.

rieben. The Sami name for fox.

rudraksha. A seed used for both Buddhist and Himalayan shamanic *malas*, or rosaries, which has protective properties. They are believed by Nepalese shamans to be created from the deity Shiva's tears in a moment of ecstasy.

runes. A northern European (Norse/Germanic) magical alphabet that predates the use of the Latin alphabet and may still be used for divination.

saiven. The Ulchi word for a spirit effigy usually made from wood.

Sami. The indigenous people of Arctic Scandinavia and the Kola Peninsula. Their traditional homeland known as Sápmi ranges across the countries of Norway, Sweden, Finland, and Russia.

San Pedro. A cactus native to the Andes Mountains of Ecuador and Peru with entheogenic (hallucinogenic) properties. The San Pedro cactus contains a number of alkaloids, including the well-studied chemical mescaline. The plant is honored by shamans of the Peruvian north coast for its ability to generate visionary and healing effects. Latin name: *Echinopsis pachanoi* (syn. *Trichocereus pachanoi*).

scrying. The art of seeing the spirits in or performing divination with a shiny/opaque surface.

seguro del curandera (curandero). A jar containing coins, small figures, talismans, symbols of the shaman's protective spirits, sweets, healing herbs, and some of the *curandera* or *curandero*'s own hair or nails, which functions as a spiritual alter ego. It is used to hold the center of the shaman's healing altar during an all-night San Pedro healing ceremony.

seiðr. A Norse divination ritual performed by women, or rarely by men, that involves a journey into the world of the deceased ancestors to receive guidance. It is performed by the *völva* whose shamanic journey is accompanied by a women's chorus.

shaman. A person who by shifting consciousness enters the spirit word to communicate with the spirits for the purpose of healing, divination, guidance, and insight. This term is usually used to designate a person with a tribal affiliation.

shamanic journey. The altered-consciousness experience of a shaman or spirit walker that allows the practitioner to interact with the enlivening essences of nature and other beings that populate the spirit realms.

shamanic state of consciousness. The state of being attained by a shaman or spirit walker while journeying, which allows them to experience the normally invisible worlds of spirit. This state may be attained through a repetitive stimulus such as drumming or rattling, chanting or dancing, as well as through the use of entheogentic compounds.

shang. A flat hand bell used by Himalayan shamans. Held in the left hand, it is used to call the spirits and to make offerings to the spirits of sound.

sieidi. Sami sacred offering place in nature. This may be a natural feature or a place constructed as a ritual space.

smudge. Ritual of fumigating with an herbal smoke for healing, clearing, or blessing a person or place.

soap nut. A plant whose dried fruits are used for washing clothes. Its seed is used in Nepal to create shamanic rosaries that cleanse the human aura. Latin name: *Sapindus mukorossi.*

spákona. A female Norse woman seer who—while in a shamanic trance—enters the roots of the great World Tree Yggdrasil to gain access to ancestral wisdom. The ritual in which this prophecy is received is known as *seiðr.* Also referred to as a *völva.*

spirit walker. A person called to the shamanic path who has developed a deep relationship with the spirits in the manner of a powerful tribal shaman. They may also be called to fill the role of shaman healer or diviner.

sweetgrass. An aromatic grass that is dried and burned as incense. Latin name: *Hierochloe odorata.*

tasso. Iron ring on a Siberian shaman's bustle.

tole. Heavy iron or bronze disk on a Siberian shaman's bustle.

tos-karak. An offering spoon used in Tuva. Rather than having one bowl as is common in a spoon used for eating, the *tos-karak* has nine wells to hold offerings of milk.

trisul. Nepalese name for the trident caried by the god Shiva, who is the primary protector of Himalayan shaman.

tsatsa. Small cast ceramic deity figure plaque used in the veneration of deities in Tibetan Buddhism and for Tibetan shamanism. *Tsatsas* may be either fired or left in an unfired state.

tupilak. An Inuit term for spirit figures that looked like monsters made from different parts of people and animals. When used for malevolent purposes, images like these could control an evil or disease-causing spirit for the purpose of causing harm.

tusakta. An Evenk traveling cap. A version of this cap may be worn as a part of a shaman's costume.

tutelary spirits. The benevolent spirits with which a spirit walker or shaman communicates.

ubaraka mri. A shaman rattle in Guarani language.

Unce Maka. A Lakota name for Mother Earth.

undee. An Ulchi processional ritual that preceeds a healing ceremony.

vajra. A Himalayan ritual object that symbolizes both the proprieties of a diamond, which is a representation of the idea of indestructibility, and a thunderbolt, which represents irresistible force. (*See also* dorje.)

Vajrakilaya. Also known as Dorje Phurba, this being is a wrathful deity who embodies the enlightened activity of all the Buddhas. This deity is able to remove obstacles, destroy the forces hostile to compassion, and purify spiritual pollution.

völ. The ritual staff of the female Norse woman seer or *völva.* Also referred to as a *seiðstafr.* It is modeled on a distaff used to hold the fiber that will be spin into yarn.

völva. A female Norse woman seer who—while in a shamanic trance—enters the roots of the great World Tree Yggdrasil to gain access to ancestral wisdom. The ritual in which this prophecy is received is known as *seiðr.* Also referred to as a *spákona.*

vorccis. The Sami term for crow.

vydutana. A Nenets term for an esteemed shaman.

World Tree. A uniting principle that connects the shamanic realms of the Upper, Middle, and Lower Worlds represented as an enormous tree. (*See also* axis mundi.)

Xam Yyash Dagyyr. Tuvan term for making a ritual offering at a shaman tree.

yalgil. The Yukaghir word for lake.

yirka-laul-vairgin. Chukchee expression that means "soft man" and refers to the male shaman whose costume resembles women's clothing.

Yggdrasil. The Norse name for the World Tree.

yompa/yampa. This is a bustle worn by Ulchi shamans. It is composed of many different pieces, each of which has its own name. These include eight- to ten-inch-long pieces of iron that have been rolled into cone-like forms, iron rods, actual bells, and in some cases ancient Chinese bronze discs with auspicious symbols cast on their faces. The iron cones which often dominate the bustle are called *kongoro;* the rods are called *kyrie;* the links are *tasso;* circular disks are referred to as *tole;* and copper bells are called *kongokto.*

Yukaghir. An eastern Siberian tribal group from the Kolyma River basin.

Yyash Dagyyr. The Tuvan ritual for sanctifying a shaman tree.

zampoña. An Andean pan flute.

Resources

Organizations

Circle of the Sacred Earth: *www.circleofthesacredearth.org*

Foundation for Shamanic Studies: *www.shamanism.org*

My Spirit Walk (source of support materials for this book): *www.myspiritwalk.com*

Nepalese Shamanism for Peace and Brotherhood (Bhola Banstola): *www.nepalese.it/en*

Shamanic Teachers and Practitioners: *www.shamanicteachers.com*

Shaman Links: *www.shamanlinks.net*

Shaman Portal: *www.shamanportal.org*

The Society for Shamanic Practitioners: *www.shamansociety.org*

Spirit Passages (author's website): *www.spiritpassages.com*

True North Health Center (The author cofounded this center in Falmouth, Maine where she offers individual shamanic healing.): *www.truenorthhealthcenter.org*

Periodicals

Sacred Hoop magazine: *www.sacredhoop.org*

Shamanic Supplies

Red Path (native-made gourd and turtle shell rattles): *www.red-path.org/native-american/dance-rattles.html*

Shaman's Market (South American shamanic practice items): *www.shamansmarket.com*

Spirit Passages (drumming and meditation CDs): *www.spiritpassages.com*

3Worlds (ritual objects for shamanism and Buddhism): *www.3worlds.co.uk*

Leather and Leather Craft Supplies

Centralia Fur and Hide (rawhide of several different species): *https://furandhide.com*

Crazy Crow Trading Port: *www.crazycrow.com/leather-supply*

Kyson Leather-Leatherhide store: *www.leatherhidestore.com*

This company has a section of remnant pieces of thin upholstery leather that are the perfect size for bag projects: www.leather-hidestore.com/servlet/the-Partial-Hides/Categories

The Leather Guy: *www.theleatherguy.org/AboutUs.aspx*

Moscow Hide and Fur (furs, bones, leather, antlers, etc.): *www.hideandfur.com*

Tandy Leather: *www.tandyleatherfactory.com/en-usd/Leather.aspx*

Waterhouse Leather: *www.waterhouseleather.com/Home.asp*

Drum Makers and Drum-making Supplies

Ancient Music (instrument makers from the UK who create drums, bone flutes, rattles, cattle horn trumpets, and stringed instruments in use before AD 1050): *www.ancientmusic.co.uk*

Cedar Mountain Drums (frame drum kits, drums, rattles, etc.): *www.cedarmtndrums.com/Catalog*

Centralia Fur and Hide (frame drum kits and supplies): *https://furandhide.com*

Nicholas Breeze Wood (amazing ritual object and drum craftsman): *www.nicholaswood.net*

Other Sites of Interest

Chapel of the Sacred Mirrors (art of Alex Grey): *www.cosm.org*

Institute of HeartMath: *www.heartmath.com*

Video Links

An Interview with Bhola Banstola: *http://youtube/9OzvRroiRMk*

Chukchi Shamanic Ritual: *http://youtube/3JJw5bTfUL8*

Shamanism in Tuva: *www.youtube.com/watch?v=nFmpWmgh LB4&feature=player_embedded*

Many other shamanic videos may be found at: *www .shamanportal.org/display_videos.php*

Notes

1   An example of a Comanche gourd rattle was included in the Denver Art Museum 1984 exhibition *Circles of the World: Traditional Art of the Plains Indians*. The catalog has a photo of this rattle on p. 118.

2   Bernard S. Mason, *Drums, Tomtoms and Rattles* (New York, NY: Dover Publications, 1974), p. 178.

3   Bradford Keeney, PhD, ed., *Guarani Shamans of the Forest* (Philadelphia, PA: Ringing Rocks Press, 2000), a book in the Profiles of Healing series.

4   Allen Wardwell, *Tangible Visions* (New York, NY: Monacelli Press, 1996), pp. 239–81.

5   The U.S. Department of the Interior, Indian Arts and Crafts Board maintains a list of Native American craftspeople as well as Native American owned and operated craft galleries and businesses. That web address is *www.doi.gov/iacb/order/source_info.html*.

6   Humphrey & Mongush & Telengid, "Attitudes to nature in Mongolia and Tuva: a preliminary report," *Nomadic Peoples* 33 (1993), p. 57 (www.nomadicpeoples.info).

7   For more details on making offerings to the spirits, read *Spirit Walking: A Course in Shamanic Power*.

8   Kenin-Lopsan, Mongush B., *Shamanic Songs and Myths of Tuva* (Budapest, Hungary: Akademiai Nyomda, 1997), p. 29.

9   More complete instructions on honoring the directions may be found in my book *Spirit Walking: A Course in Shamanic Power*.

10 Sandra Harner, PhD, and Warren W. Tryon, "Psychological and Immunological Responses to Shamanic Journeying with Drumming," *SHAMAN* 4, Nos. 1-2 (1996).

11 Sandra Harner, PhD, "Shamanism and the Immune Response," Exploring the Frontiers of Consciousness Lecture series, Institute of Noetic Science; San Francisco: June 26, 2002. From a CD recording of the lecture produced by the Foundation for Shamanic Studies, Mill Valley, CA © 2002.

12 Ibid.

13 Ye. D. Prokofyeva, "The Costume of an Enets Shaman," in *Studies in Siberian Shamanism*, edited by Henry N. Michael (Toronto, Canada: University of Toronto Press for the Arctic Institute of North America, 1963), p. 147.

14 Ibid, p. 148.

15 Video "Nganasan Shamanism" (Mill Valley, CA: Foundation for Shamanic Studies, 1999) edited from the original footage from the 1978 expedition by A. Oskin and Y. Simchenko, Russian Academy of Sciences: Institute of Ethnology and Anthropology.

16 M.A. Czaplicka, *Aboriginal Siberia, A Study in Social Anthropology* (London: Oxford University Press, 1969; reprint of the original 1914 edition), p. 209.

17 Lauri Vahtre, Jüri Viikberg, Ants Viires, PhD, and others, *The Red Book of the Peoples of the Russian Empire* (Estonia, 1992). Information taken from the online version of this book available at *www.eki.ee/books/redbook/*.

18 S. Ia. Serov, "Guardians and Spirit-masters of Siberia," in *Crossroads of Continents* (Washington, DC: Smithsonian Institution, 1988), photo p. 241.

19 Joan Halifax, *Shaman: The Wounded Healer* (London: Thames & Hudson, 1992), p. 50.

20 Ekaterina Devlet, "Rock art and the material culture of Siberian and Central Asian shamanism," in *The Archaeology of Shamanism* edited by Neil Price (London and New York; Routledge/Taylor & Francis Group, 2001), p. 45.

21 Halifax, *Shaman: The Wounded Healer*, p. 51.

22 Czaplicka, *Aboriginal Siberia, A Study in Social Anthropology*, p. 207.

23 Wardwell, *Tangible Visions*, pp. 236–37.

24 Foundation for Shamanic Studies, *Drums of the Ancestors*, video of their 1996 expedition to China.

25 Nathan Muus, "The Sami Drum," *Baiki, The North American Sami Journal* 17 (Winter 1998), p. 8.

26 Southern Alaskan elder Martha Demientieff was quoted in the description of a 19th-century shaman's whistle used in the National Museum of Natural History, Smithsonian Institution exhibit *Looking Both Ways*.

27 A video of the reproduction Divje Babe flute being played may be found at *www.youtube.com/watch?v=sHy9FOblt7Y*. The research on the flute is available on *www.cpa.si/ tidldibab.pdf*.

28 Transfiguration is a term used by Sandra Ingerman in her *Medicine for the Earth* work to describe the state when a practitioner's perceptions of form are released to unveil her or his radiant light body.

29 An article on *malas* that includes this divination process may be found in issue 56 of *Sacred Hoop* magazine. A copy of this article is available at *www.3worlds.co.uk/Articles/Mala.pdf*.

30 A complete description of the Phi Faa ritual was published by Warawut Roengbuthra and Bussakorn Sumrongthong (2006), "Phi Faa Ritual Music of the Northeastern Part of Thailand," *Voices: A World Forum for Music Therapy*.

Retrieved June 24, 2012, from *www.voices.no/mainissues/ mi40006000200.html*.

31 Details about the grave and its occupant may be found at *http://anthropology.net/2008/11/04/a-12000-year-old-shaman-from-hilazon-tachtit-israel-the-emergence-of-religion*.

32 The contents of this grave are preserved in the Mesolithic Period Permanent Collection of the Landesamt für Denkmalpflege und Archäologie Sachsen-Anhalt. The English version of the website is *www.lda-lsa.de/en/state_museum_of_prehistory/ permanent_exhibition/mesolithic_period/*.

33 An extensive description of a *curandero's mesa* may be found in Eduardo Calderón, Richard Cowan, Douglas Sharon, F. Kaye Sharon, *Eduardo el Curandero: The Words of a Peruvian Healer* (Richmond, CA: North Atlantic Books, 1982).

34 Instructions for creating a *despacho* may be found in my book *Spirit Walking: A Course in Shamanic Power*.

35 Czaplicka, *Aboriginal Siberia, A Study in Social Anthropology*, p. 226.

36 An excellent article on this subject by Nicholas Breeze Wood—the publisher of *Sacred Hoop* magazine—may be found at *www.3worlds.co.uk/Articles/Shamans-Mirrors.pdf*.

37 Dmitri Nagishin, *Folktales of the Amur: Stories from the Russian Far East* (New York: Harry N. Abrams, Inc.,1980), pp.182–92.

38 I learned this directly from Grandfather Misha. You may read more about his use of smoke in Roberta Louis's article "Shamanic Healing Practices of the Ulchi," published in *Shaman's Drum Magazine* (No. 53, Fall 1999). While Grandfather Misha did not use a feather to move the smoke, the same purpose was served by a small brush created from larch shavings.

39 Calderón, Cowan, Douglas Sharon, F. Kaye Sharon, *Eduardo el Curandero: The Words of a Peruvian Healer*, pp.86–99.

40 Wardwell, *Tangible Visions*, pp. 218–33.

41 Prokofyeva, "The Costume of an Enets Shaman," pp. 124–56.

42 Karen Kelly, "Thorbjorg's Story, An Introduction to Seiðr," *Spirit Talk* 9 (Early Summer 1999). *Spirit Talk* is an online core-shamanic newsletter which is available at *www.shamaniccircles.org/spirit_talk*.

43 Czaplicka, *Aboriginal Siberia, A Study in Social Anthropology*, p. 365.

44 Ibid, p. 199.

45 Foundation for Shamanic Studies, *Drums of the Ancestors*.

46 Czaplicka, *Aboriginal Siberia, A Study in Social Anthropology*, pp. 211–15.

47 Ibid, p. 211.

48 Ibid, p. 199.

49 Ibid, p. 210.

50 Foundation for Shamanic Studies, *Drums of the Ancestors*.

51 Czaplicka, *Aboriginal Siberia, A Study in Social Anthropology*, p. 219.

52 Wardwell, *Tangible Visions* , pp. 282–92.

53 Czaplicka, *Aboriginal Siberia, A Study in Social Anthropology*, p. 215.

54 Ibid, p. 219.

55 Wardwell, *Tangible Visions*, pp. 212–17.

56 Czaplicka, *Aboriginal Siberia, A Study in Social Anthropology*, p. 203.

57 Mikhailowski is a Russian anthropologist whose work Czaplicka refers to in her book.

58 Morris, James Cheston, "Relation Of The Pentagonal Dodecahedron Found Near Marietta, Ohio, To Shamanism: Discussion And Remarks On Shamanism" (1897).

Bibliography

Calderón, Eduardo, Richard Cowan, Douglas Sharon, and F. Kaye Sharon. *Eduardo el Curandero: The Words of a Peruvian Healer.* Richmond, CA; North Atlantic Books, 1982.

Castaneda, Carlos. *The Teachings of Don Juan: A Yaqui Way of Knowledge.* New York, NY: Washington Square Press, 1968.

Czaplicka, M. A. *Aboriginal Siberia, A Study in Social Anthropology.* London: Oxford University Press, 1969 reprint of the original 1914 edition.

Devlet, Ekaterina. "Rock art and the material culture of Siberian and Central Asian shamanism." In *The Archaeology of Shamanism,* p. 45, edited by Neil Price. London and New York, NY: Routledge/Taylor & Francis Group, 2001.

Eliade, Mircea. *Shamanism: Archaic Techniques of Ecstasy.* New Jersey: Princeton University Press, 1964.

Fedorova, Natalia. "Bronze castings of western Siberia." In *The Archaeology of Shamanism,* edited by Neil Price. London and New York, NY: Routledge/Taylor & Francis Group, 2001.

Foundation for Shamanic Studies Video. *Drums of the Ancestors* (1996 expedition to China). Mill Valley, CA: Foundation for Shamanic Studies, 1997.

————. *Nganasan Shamanism.* Mill Valley, CA: Foundation for Shamanic Studies, 1999. Edited from the original footage from the 1978 expedition by A. Oskin and Y. Simchenko, Russian Academy of Sciences: Institute of Ethnology and Anthropology.

Halifax, Joan. *Shaman: The Wounded Healer.* London: Thames Hudson, 1992.

Harner, Michael, PhD. *The Way of the Shaman.* New York, NY: HarperCollins Publishers, 1990 edition.

————. Interview reprinted in *Shaman's Drum Magazine*, Number 71.

Harner, Sandra, PhD. "Shamanism and the Immune Response." Exploring the Frontiers of Consciousness Lecture Series. Institute of Noetic Science; San Francisco: June 26, 2002. From a CD recording of the lecture produced by The Foundation For Shamanic Studies, Mill Valley, CA 2002.

Harner, Sandra, PhD, and Warren W. Tryon. "Psychological and Immunological Responses to Shamanic Journeying with Drumming." *SHAMAN* 4, Nos. 1–2, 1996.

Hunt, W. Ben. *The Complete How-to Book of Indiancraft.* New York, NY: Macmillian Publishing Co. 1973.

Joralemon, Donald, and Douglas Sharon. *Sorcery and Shamanism.* Salt Lake City, UT: University of Utah Press, 1993.

Kelly, Karen. "Thorbjorg's Story, An Introduction to Seiðr." *Spirit Talk* 9 (Early Summer 1999). *Spirit Talk* is an online core-shamanic newsletter available at *www.shamaniccircles.org/spirit_talk*.

Louis, Roberta. "Shamanic Healing Practices of the Ulchi." *Shaman's Drum Magazine* 53 (Fall 1999).

Mason, Bernard S. *Drums, Tomtoms and Rattles.* New York, NY: Dover Publications, 1974.

McClenon, James, PhD. "The Experiential Foundations of Shamanic Healing." *Journal of Medicine and Philosophy* 18 (1993): 107–27.

Muus, Nathan. "The Sami Drum." *Baiki, The North American Sami Journal* 17 (Winter 1998).

Nagishin, Dmitri. *Folktales of the Amur: Stories from the Russian Far East.* New York, NY: Harry N. Abrams, Inc.1980.

Petrovic, Boris. "Overtone-Singing/Throat-Singing." *www.docstoc.com/docs/21849609/Overtone-Singing-Throat-Singing* accessed September 30, 2010.

Prokofyeva, Ye. D. "The Costume of an Enets Shaman." In *Studies in Siberian Shamanism*, edited by Henry N. Michael. Toronto: University of Toronto Press for the Arctic Institute of North America, 1963.

Rysdyk, Evelyn C. *Spirit Walking: A Course in Shamanic Power.* San Francisco, CA; Red Wheel/Weiser, Inc., 2013.

Serov, S. Ia. "Guardians and Spirit-masters of Siberia." In *Crossroads of Continents.* Washington, DC: Smithsonian Institution, 1988.

Shepard, Paul, and Barry Sanders. *The Sacred Paw, The Bear in Nature, Myth and Literature.* New York, NY: Viking Penguin, Inc., 1985.

Tedlock, Barbara, PhD. *The Woman in the Shaman's Body.* New York, NY: Bantam Dell, 2005.

Vitebsky, Piers, PhD. *The Shaman.* Boston, New York, NY: Little Brown and Company, 1995.

Wardwell, Allen. *Tangible Visions.* New York, NY: Monacelli Press, 1996.

Winkelman, Michael. "Trance States: A Theoretical Model and Cross-Cultural Analysis." *Ethos* 14, No. 2 (Summer, 1986): 174–203. Published by Blackwell Publishing on behalf of the American Anthropological Association; stable URL *www.jstor.org/stable/639951* accessed: 30/03/2010 16:03.

Wood, Nicholas Breeze. "Mirrors of the Soul: The use of Metal Mirrors in Asian Shamanism." *Sacred Hoop Magazine* (Spring 2005). An Internet version is available at *www.3worlds.co.uk/Articles/Shamans-Mirrors.pdf.*

———. *Voices From the Earth: Practical Shamanism.* New York, NY: Sterling Publishing Co., 2000.

About the Author

Evelyn C. Rysdyk is a shamanic practitioner and teacher. She has studied with Michael Harner and Sandra Ingerman and is a graduate of the Foundation for Shamanic Studies Three-Year Program in Advanced Shamanism and Shamanic Healing. Since that time, she has worked with indigenous shamans from Siberia, Peru, Central Asia and Nepal. Evelyn helped found True North, an integrated medical center in Falmouth, Maine, where she works alongside medical practitioners to bring physical, spiritual, emotional, and spiritual healing to patients. She lives in Maine. Visit her at *www.evelynrysdyk.com.*

To Our Readers

Weiser Books, an imprint of Red Wheel/Weiser, publishes books across the entire spectrum of occult, esoteric, speculative, and New Age subjects. Our mission is to publish quality books that will make a difference in people's lives without advocating any one particular path or field of study. We value the integrity, originality, and depth of knowledge of our authors.

Our readers are our most important resource, and we appreciate your input, suggestions, and ideas about what you would like to see published.

Visit our website at *www.redwheelweiser.com* to learn about our upcoming books and free downloads, and be sure to go to www.redwheelweiser.com/newsletter to sign up for newsletters and exclusive offers.

You can also contact us at *info@rwwbooks.com* or at

Red Wheel/Weiser, LLC
665 Third Street, Suite 400
San Francisco, CA 94107